SECRETS

OF

DULCE

KEN HUDNALL

**OMEGA PRESS
EL PASO, TX**

SECRETS OF DULCE
COPYRIGHT © 2015 KEN HUDNALL

All rights reserved. No part of this book may be reproduced or transmitted in any form or by any means, graphic, electronic, or mechanical, including photocopying, recording, taping or by any information storage or retrieval system, without the permission in writing from the publisher.

OMEGA PRESS
An imprint of Omega Communications Group, Inc.

For information contact:

Omega Press

5823 N. Mesa, #839

El Paso, Texas 79912

Or http://www.kenhudnall.com

FIRST EDITION
Printed in the United States of America

OTHER WORKS BY THE SAME AUTHOR FROM OMEGA PRESS

MANHATTAN CONSPIRACY SERIES
Blood on the Apple
Capitol Crimes
Angel of Death

THE OCCULT CONNECTION
UFOs, Secret Societies and Ancient Gods
The Hidden Race
Flying Saucers
UFOs and the Supernatural
UFOs and Secret Societies
UFOs and Ancient Gods
Evidence of Alien Contact
Sensual Alien Encounters

SHADOW WARS
Shadow Rulers

DARKNESS
When Darkness Falls
Fear The Darkness

SPIRITS OF THE BORDER
(with Connie Wang)
The History and Mystery of El Paso Del Norte
The History and Mystery of Fort Bliss, Texas

(with Sharon Hudnall)
The History and Mystery of the Rio Grande
The history and Mystery of New Mexico
The History and Mystery of the Lone Star State

The History and Mystery of Arizona
The History and Mystery of Tombstone, AZ
The History and Mystery of Colorado
Echoes of the Past
El Paso: A City of Secrets
Tales From The Nightshift
The History and Mystery of Sin City
The History and Mystery of Concordia
Military Ghosts
Restless Spirits
School Spirits
Nautical Ghosts

THE ESTATE SALE MURDERS
Dead Man's Diary

OTHER WORKS

Northwood Conspiracy

No Safe Haven; Homeland Insecurity

Where No Car Has Gone Before

Seventy Years and No Losses:

The History of the Sun Bowl

How Not To Get Published

Vampires, Werewolves and Things
That Go Bump In The Night

Even Paranoids Have Enemies

Criminal Law for Laymen

Understanding Business Law

Language of the Law

The Border Escapades of Billy the Kid

PUBLISHED BY PAJA BOOKS
The Occult Connection: Unidentified Flying Objects

DEDICATION
As with all of my books, I could not have completed this book if not for my lovely wife, Sharon. Additionally, I want to thank Chief Raynard Faber and the memebrs of the Jicarrilla Apache Tribe.

TABLE OF CONTENTS

- CHAPTER ONE 9
- DULCE, NEW MEXICO 9
- PART ONE 17
- DULCE BASE 17
- CHAPTER TWO 19
- HOME OF A SECRET UNDERGROUND BASE 19
- CHAPTER THREE 27
- INVOLVEMENT OF PAUL BENNEWITZ 27
- CHAPTER FOUR 35
- ARCHULETA MESA 35
- CHAPTER FIVE 53
- WHAT IS KNOWN ABOUT THE DULCE LAB 53
- CHAPTER SIX 75
- THE DULCE WARS 75
- CHAPTER SEVEN 95
- A MYSTERIOUS DEATH 95
- PART TWO 105
- STRANGE CREATURES 105
- CHAPTER EIGHT 107
- CREATURES OF THE NIGHT 107
- CHAPTER NINE 119
- OTHER TUNNELS 119
- CHAPTER TEN 125
- AN INTERESTING INTERVIEW 125
- CHAPTER ELEVEN 173
- IS IT REAL? 173
- INDEX 221

CHAPTER ONE

DULCE, NEW MEXICO

Figure 1: A member of the Jicarilla Nation

On its face, the community of Dulce is nothing special. Dulce is a census-designated place (CDP) in Rio Arriba County, New Mexico, United States. The population was 2,623 at the 2000 census, almost entirely Native American. It is the largest community and tribal headquarters of the Jicarilla Apache Reservation. According to the United States Census Bureau, the CDP has a total area of 12.9 square miles, all of it land.

As of the census of 2000, there were 2,623 people, 779 households, and 595 families residing in the CDP. The population density was 202.6 people per square mile. There were 899 housing units at an average density of 69.4 per square mile (26.8/km²). The racial makeup of the CDP is 3.43% White, 0.04% African American, 90.66% Native American, 4.35% from other races, and 1.52% from two or more races. Hispanic or Latino of any race was 11.74% of the population.

There were 779 households out of which 48.7% had children under the age of 18 living with them, 38.8% were married couples living together, 28.9% had a female householder with no husband present, and 23.6% were non-families. 19.9% of all households were made up of individuals and 5.3% had someone living alone who was 65 years of age or older. The average household size was 3.34 and the average family size was 3.83.

In the CDP the population was spread out with 40.0% under the age of 18, 10.0% from 18 to 24, 29.2% from 25 to 44, 16.3% from 45 to 64, and 4.6% who were 65 years of age or older. The median age was 25 years. For every 100 females there were 92.3 males. For every 100 females age 18 and over, there were 91.4 males.

The median income for a household in the CDP was $26,818, and the median income for a family was $29,402. Males had a median income of $26,055 versus $21,623 for females. The per capita income for the CDP was $10,108. About 24.8% of families and 29.5% of the population were below the poverty line, including 34.6% of those under age 18 and 41.4% of those ages 65 or over. Children from Dulce attend the schools of ISD 21, which has a total enrollment of approximately 650 students from kindergarten through high school.

Figure 2: the land around Dulce is rugged.

Before discussing some of the mysteries and secrets of this area, we need to take a look at those who live there. Jicarilla Apache refers to the members of the Jicarilla Apache Nation currently living in New Mexico and speaking a Southern Athabaskan language. The term Jicarilla, pronounced "hick-ah-REE-uh", comes from Mexican Spanish meaning "little basket". Their autonym is Tinde or Dinde, meaning "the People". To neighboring

Apache bands like the Mescalero and Lipan they were known as Kinya-Inde ("People who live in fixed houses"). The Jicarilla called themselves also Haisndayin translated as "people who came from below", because they believed that they were the sole descendants of the first people to emerge from the underworld, the abode of Ancestral Man and Ancestral Woman who produced the first people[1].

    The Jicarilla Apache lived in a semi-nomadic existence in the Sangre de Cristo Mountains and plains of southern Colorado, northern New Mexico and ranged into the Great Plains starting before 1525 CE. They lived a relatively peaceful life for years, traveling seasonally to traditional hunting, gathering and cultivation along river beds. The Jicarilla learned about farming and pottery from the Puebloan peoples and learned about survival on the plains from the Plains Indians and had a rich and varied diet and lifestyle. Starting in the 1700s Colonial New Spain, pressure from other Native American tribes, like the Comanches, and later westward expansion of the United States resulted in significant loss of property, removal from their sacred lands, and relocation to lands not suited for survival.

---

[1] Tiller, Veronica E. Velarde, The Jicarilla Apache Tribe: A History, BowArrow Publishing Company, Albuquerque, NM. 2000.

The mid-1800s until the mid-1900s were particularly difficult as tribal bands were displaced, treaties were made and broken, and subject to significant loss of life due to tuberculosis and other diseases, and lack of opportunities for survival. By 1887 they received their reservation, which was expanded in 1907 to include land more conducive to ranching and agriculture, and within several decades realized the rich natural resources of the San Juan Basin under the reservation land.

Tribal members transitioned from a semi-nomadic lifestyle and are now supported by their oil and gas, casino

Figure 3: The Great Seal of the Jicarilla Nation.

gaming, forestry, ranching and tourism industries on the reservation. The Jicarilla continue to be known for their pottery, basketry and beadwork.

In 2013, I spent several days exploring Dulce and the surrounding area as the guest of Chief Raynard Faber and then I went back again in late 2013 to take some additional photos. The people who live there are friendly, though they do tend to be somewhat clannish at first glance. However, once they know you, they are friendly and open and exclude a great pride about their history, traditions and home. Some of the information that came out in interviews had been kept quit for years. I think when you have read this material you will agree with me that the Dulce area hides secrets that could change the world if known.

During my visits to Dulce I also found that the locals know a whole lot more than they let on to outsiders. The locals know the secrets of Dulce that we will discuss here as well as many more. In addition to the many stories of there being a secret

Figure 4: A Sasquatch also known as a Bigfoot.

underground alien base located on Archuleta Mesa, there are numerous stories of sightings of Sasquatch as well as other creatures of the night.

PART ONE

DULCE BASE

CHAPTER TWO

HOME OF A SECRET UNDERGROUND BASE

For many years there have been numerous stories about mysteries related to Dulce, New Mexico and the surrounding area. One of the best known stories to come out of Dulce is the existence of a secret underground base that is supposed to be jointly manned by U.S. troops and alien beings under a treaty worked out in the 1950s.

The history of this secret base in inextricably tied to the story of Paul Bennewitz. Starting in 1979, Bennewitz became convinced he was intercepting electronic communications from alien spacecraft and installations outside of Albuquerque. By the 1980s he believed he had discovered an underground base near Dulce. The story spread rapidly within the UFO community and by 1990, Ufologist John Lear claimed he had independent confirmations of the base's existence.

Political scientist Michael Barkun wrote that the existence of Cold War underground missile installations in the area gave superficial plausibility to the rumors, making the Dulce base story an "attractive legend" within Ufology. According to Barkun, claims about experiments on abductees and firefights between aliens and the Delta Force place the Dulce legend "well outside even the most far-fetched reports of secret underground bases."[2]

The Dulce, New Mexico Base

According to the many stories circulating about an underground Military Base/Laboratory in Dulce, New Mexico it connects with the underground network of tunnels which honeycombs our planet. The base extends many hundreds of feet into the earth and the lower levels of this base are allegedly under the control of Inner Earth beings or Aliens.

This base is connected to Los Alamos research facilities via an underground "tube-shuttle" that connects to many known as well as unknown bases located throughout

---

[2] Wikipedia

the North American Continent. (It can be assumed that such a shuttle way would be a straight-line construction. It should then be possible, by using maps and some deduction, to determine the most likely location of this base, especially since the general location is already known.)

The creation of this alleged underground base was undertaken about the same time as the crash of a UFO in Roswell, New Mexico. It would be interesting to determine if in fact there was an actual connection. There are those who believe that the UFO that crashed in Roswell was enroute to the Dulce base.

Beginning in 1947, a road was built near the Dulce Base, under the cover of a lumber company needing to gain access to the large amount of uncut timber in and around Dulce. It should be noted that though the road in question was built at great expense, little if any cut timber was ever hauled out of the dense forests surrounding the town of Dulce. Sometime after the creation of this timber road was completed, it was inexplicably destroyed.

Navajo Dam is the Dulce Base's main source of power, though there is a second source of available power in El Vado (which is said to be another hidden entrance to the underground base.). (Note: The above facts should also help searchers to locate the general location of the base.) Most of the lakes near Dulce and a lot of other unexplained work in and around the area of the supposed underground base were made using government grants "for" the Indians. There are those who have claimed that the many miles of tunnels that would be required for such an undertaking would be impossible to construct. However, the specialized equipment for such an undertaking has been in existence for some time[3]. The grant request documentation which explained and justified the need for these projects on the Jicarilla Reservation cannot be found.

Bechtel (BECK-tul) a super-secret international corporate conglomerate, founded in 1898 was given the job of actually building the Dulce base. Some say the firm is really a 'Shadow Government's working arm of the CIA. But whatever it is called, Bechtel is the largest Construction and Engineering outfit in the U.S.A and the World (and some say, beyond)." It should also be noted that it is said that the most important posts in U.S.A. Government are

---

[3] Note: The September, 1983 issue of Omni (Pg. 80) has a color drawing of 'The Subterrene,' the Los Alamos nuclear-powered tunnel machine that burrows through the rock, deep underground, by heating whatever stone it encounters into molten rock, which cools after the Subterrene has moved on. The result is a tunnel with a smooth, glazing lining.)"

held by former Bechtel Officers[4]. Also keep in mind that throughout the Bush wars Bechtel was given first choice of projects in the rebuilding of Iraq and Afghanistan which generated many billions of dollars in revenue for the company.

Locals have reported that there are over 100 Secret Exits near and around Dulce. Some are located in and around Archuleta Mesa which towers of the small town, while others can be found around Dulce Lake and even as far east as Lindrich. Some deep sections of the Complex connect into several natural Cavern Systems.

This base is designed to be almost entirely self-sufficient and was built with state of the art technology. For example, the elevators, lights, and doors at Dulce Base are all magnetically controlled[5].

It should also be noted that the area around Dulce has had a high number of reported Animal Mutilations. The researchers at Dulce Base have also abducted several people from Dulce's civilian population and implanted devices of various types in their heads and bodies[6]. It

---

[4] Keep in mind that former Vice President Dick Cheney was a former Bechtel official.
[5] Information sent to author by an individual known as Yellow Fruit.
[6] It is said that when Livermore Berkeley Labs began producing blood for the Dulce Base in the mid-1980s, the occurrence of Human and Animal abductions slowed considerably.

should also be noted that numerous abductees such as Christa Tilton reported being taken to the Dulce Base when they were abducted.

Security Arrangements

One of the benefits the aliens received from the treaty that they entered into with the U.S. government was U.S. furnished security. Certainly guards of such a hybrid facility could not be taken from the general rank and file of the military. Rather such duty is the exclusive purview of units such as Delta Group. DELTA group (from the National Recon Group) is responsible for security of all Alien-connected projects. The DELTA symbol is a Black Triangle on a Red Background.

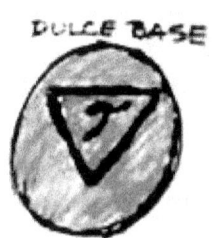

Figure 5: Dulce Base's Symbol

Dulce Base's symbol is a Delta (triangle) with the Greek Letter "Tau" (t) within it, and then the entire symbol is inverted, so the triangle points down, and the "Tau" is also inverted[7].

During this author's Sasquatch hunt in the Four Corners Region of New Mexico

---

[7] Christa Tilton was an abductee who claimed that she was taken to Dulce Base) She is the editor of "Crux" magazine, which deals with UFOs, abductions, etc. P.O. Box 906237 Tulsa, Oklahoma.

numerous interviews were conducted with locals who mentioned coming in contact with black clad men carrying M-16s and M4s. They would chase the locals away with threats of death, arrest and incarceration.

One or two interviewees reported finding mobile command posts in the thick timber that contained maps and other information. Unfortunately, through the command posts were initially empty; security quickly arrived to chase the away as if they had tripped some alarm system.

CHAPTER THREE

INVOLVEMENT OF PAUL BENNEWITZ

As mentioned earlier, much of the initial information about the Dulce Base came from Paul Bennewitz.

Figure 6: Paul Bennewitz

To examine the Paul Bennewitz involvement, we must first start with the premise that the Dulce Base is an alleged secret alien underground facility located underneath Archuleta Mesa on the Colorado-New Mexico border near the town of Dulce, New Mexico. The initial claims of alien activity there were first publicized by Albuquerque businessman Paul Bennewitz, though many others soon arrived to support his claims. As the reader might guess this information hit the UFO community like a ton of bricks.

Paul Frederic Bennewitz, Jr. (September 29, 1927 - June 23, 2003) was an American businessman and UFO investigator who originated stori4es of a number of UFO Conspiracies in the 1980s. He was a son of Paul Frederic Bennewitz, Sr. (1900-1949) and Stella A. Sharp.

A one-time PhD candidate in physics, Bennewitz produced a great deal of information supporting the existence of a plot involving an extensive network of UFO bases tied to an alien colonization and a control scheme to subjugate the human race. After he saw the hypnosis sessions of Myrna Hansen[8], who claimed to have UFO

---

[8] 28 year old Myrna Hansen & her 6 year old son saw five UFOs descend into a cow pasture as they were driving home near Cimarron, N. M. on May 5, 1980. Afterwards she had a period of missing time of 4 hours, and confused memories of an alien abduction. She later was hypnotically regressed on May 11 & June 3.

According to her account, while under hypnosis, two figures in white suits emerged from one of the UFOs and mutilated one of the cows in the field, while the animal was still alive, using an 18" knife. She & her son were captured and taken to separate ships. She resisted but was undressed and given a physical examination. The exam was interrupted by a tall human who apologized and ordered the aliens punished. He then took Hansen on a tour of this and possibly other craft. The last UFO took flight as she was next lead into a landscape

experiences, he became convinced that the wave of cattle mutilations throughout the Southwest were due to alien involvement. Bennewitz claimed that as a result of his research he had uncovered evidence of aliens controlling humans through electromagnetic devices, and he also claimed that UFOs were regularly flying near Kirtland Air Force Base and the nearby Manzano Nuclear Weapons Storage Facility and Coyote Canyon Test Area.

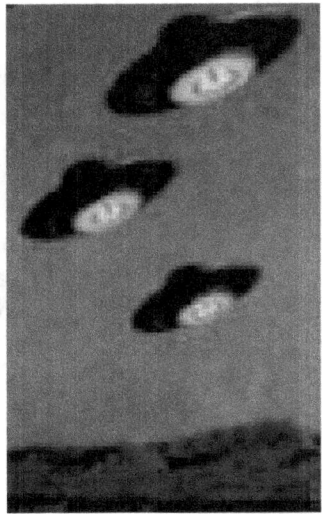

Figure 7: UFOs that are seen above many cities

Convinced that he was intercepting electronic communications originating from alien spacecraft located outside of Albuquerque, New Mexico, Bennewitz soon believed that he had located a secret alien facility that he called Dulce Base. By 1982, Bennewitz began to spread his

---

that she believed was west of Las Cruces, N.M. and another near Roswell, N.M. She was then taken into an underground base where she managed to escape briefly. She found herself in a room full of what appeared to be tanks and discovered human body parts floating in them.

Hansen was dragged out of that area and she and her son were put through a painful process involving loud noises and blinding lights before they were taken back aboard the UFO & flown, with her car aboard too, back to the site of the abduction.

ideas regarding Dulce Base to others in the Ufology community. In 1988 he wrote a paper entitled "Project Beta" detailing how the base might be successfully attacked.

Bennewitz detailed his assertions to the Aerial Phenomena Research Organization (APRO), who regarded him as a deluded paranoid. Ufologist William Moore[9], who later confessed to having been a disinformation agent working for the government, claims that he tried to push Bennewitz, who had been in a mental health facility on three occasions after suffering severe delusional paranoia, into a mental breakdown by intentionally feeding him false information about aliens. Former special agent for the U.S. Air Force Office of Special Investigations Richard Doty claimed that in the 1980s he was tasked with hoaxing documents and feeding false information to UFO researchers, including Bennewitz. However, the question becomes was it a true disinformation program or were these actions taken to cover up the fact that real information regarding the Dulce Base was being released and Bennewitz had to be discredited. Either was a possibility.

---

[9] William Leonard Moore (born October 31, 1943) is an author and former UFO researcher, prominent from the late 1970s to the late 1980s. He co-authored two books with Charles Berlitz, including The Roswell Incident.

It later came out that starting in 1979 Bennewitz became convinced he was intercepting electronic communications from alien spacecraft and installations outside of Albuquerque. By the 1980s he believed he had discovered an underground base near Dulce. The story spread rapidly within the UFO community and by 1990, Ufologist John Lear[10] claimed he had independent confirmations of the base's existence.

Political scientist Michael Barkun[11] believed that Cold War underground missile installations in the area gave

---

[10] John Lear is a retired airline captain and former CIA pilot, as well as the son of the famous inventor of the Lear Jet. He is a former Lockheed L-1011 Captain and is highly regarded in aviation circles. He has flown over 150 aircraft and has earned every certificate granted by the Federal Aviation Administration. John also held 18 world speed records and has worked for 28 different Aircraft Corporations. During the late 1980s and early 1990s, John began coming forward with some startling revelations concerning the subject of aerial phenomena and Unidentified Flying Objects.

[11] Michael Barkun (born April 8, 1938) is professor emeritus of political science at the Maxwell School of Citizenship and Public Affairs, Syracuse University, specializing in political extremism and the relationship between religion and violence. He is the author of a number of books on the subject, including Religion and The Racist Right: The Origins of the Christian Identity Movement (1996), A Culture of Conspiracy: Apocalyptic Visions in Contemporary America (2003) and Chasing Phantoms: Reality, Imagination, and Homeland Security Since 9/11 (2011).

Barkun has acted as a consultant for the Federal Bureau of Investigation; as a member of the Special Advisory Commission to the FBI's Critical Incident Response Group in 1995–1996, he provided training and background presentations on the radical right] He serves on the editorial boards of Terrorism and Political Violence and Nova Religio, and was the editor of Communal Societies from 1987 to 1994.

superficial plausibility to the rumors, making the Dulce base story an "attractive legend" within Ufology. According to Barkun, claims about experiments on abductees and firefights between aliens and the Delta Force place the Dulce legend "well outside even the most far-fetched reports of secret underground bases."

The story of the Dulce base was even featured in an episode of the History Channel program *UFO Hunters*. The show's investigators traveled to Dulce to conduct interviews and visit the Archuleta Mesa where the base is reportedly hidden. It was also featured in an episode of *Conspiracy Theory* with Jesse Ventura. *Ancient Aliens* Season 2, Episode 4, had a short segment talking about the brief history of the alleged Dulce Base and its impact on the Jicarilla Native American Culture.

This author has been interested in the UFO mystery since the 1960s and I have read almost everything I could get my hands on about the topic. Additionally over the last 50 or so years I have talked to a number of people who have had contact with the occupants of those mysterious flying lights. My first radio show, called Adventure

---

He edits the Religion and Politics book series for the Syracuse University Press. He won the 2003 Distinguished Scholar award from the Communal Studies Association, and the Myers Center Award for the Study of Human Rights for his book Religion and the Racist Right. He earned his Ph.D. from Northwestern University in 1965.

Radio[12], had a large content regarding UFOs, aliens and secret underground bases. In this book, I am taking what I was told on my show and putting it together with some of the writings of researchers I consider competent.

Now of course, all of the material circulating about secret basis cannot be verified. If it could then the bases would not be secret and Congress would be called on the carpet to explain secret treaties with aliens. Most of what I am going to discuss is actually third party information which has been collected from supposed Dulce personnel, construction workers who were employed there, inner-Earth researchers and former abductees.

---

[12] KHRO Radio, Anaheim, CA.

CHAPTER FOUR

ARCHULETA MESA

Archuleta Mesa is the central geographic feature of Dulce, New Mexico, the heart of the Jicarilla Apache Nation. There is tribal government housing, a casino and hotel, one grocery store, and after the stand-off shootout that happened at the Philip's 66, there's only one gas station. The main center of activity is Wild Horse Casino, the small casino/restaurant in town. The people are reserved but once introduced by someone they know, they are friendly and helpful. In 2009, 120 people attended the Dulce Underground UFO Base Conference.

Figure 8: Entrance to Wild Horse Casino

Once the locals could be coaxed into discussing the odd happenings in the area, there were numerous stories told of strange creatures, black helicopters and lights in the sky. Some expressed lingering fear, and some treated the events as just part of living in Dulce, however, everyone had an opinion as to what they were and where they came from.

During my Sasquatch Hunt[13], I was introduced by Chief Raynard Faber to numerous individuals living and working in the area from Dulce to Lumberton, New Mexico

---

[13] There will soon be both a video as well as a book on this Sasquatch hunt. Watch for them.

to just over the state line in Colorado[14]. Some claimed that it was all a hoax, yet many claim to have seen strange and bizarre sights such as coyotes that turn into humans, big orbs of light floating in the valleys, dogs that run faster than a speeding car, Bigfoot, cow fetuses with the face of a tiger—and aliens, specifically, the Greys. In addition to these I was also treated to a litany of stories about black uniformed armed men who could go through the thickest timber and underbrush without making a sound of leaving a trail as well as numerous stories of black, unmarked helicopters coming and going from the top of Archuleta Mesa.

During my first meal at the Casino, I was introduced to a couple who warmly welcomed me to their community. When Chief Faber told them that I was there chasing Sasquatch, the husband smiled and asked what I thought about aliens and UFOs. When I told him that I had written several books on UFOs he proceeded to tell me a story about what had happened to a group of women in the area.

---

[14] My visit to the hot springs in Colorado was the result of a fall on the ice which caused a back injury. From the moment that I arrived in Dulce it snowed constantly and the ice built up was a real danger to drivers and even walkers.

He said that there was a group of ladies who had gone to some type of religious conference over in Farmington, New Mexico[15]. The conference had lasted all day and it was quite late as they drove home. As it was so late, there was little traffic and no stores were open along the way so it was rather dark.

Suddenly, directly in their path in the middle of the road an image took shape in the middle of the road. The creature was a biped (it had two feet) and it was somewhat taller than the average human. Extending out of the torso was what appeared to be a long thick tale covered in gray scales swaying back and forth across the width of the road.

Rather than stop, the driver swerved to swerve to miss the creature. As they went past it, all of them saw that it had the face of a reptile. Later when they told someone what had happened they were told that the creature was probably a reptilian Grey, one of the two types of aliens that live in the tunnels and seven-level military base underneath Archuleta Mountain. They are bipeds, have scales and sometimes appear like radiant beings.

---

[15] I have written about some of the strange things that have happened in Farmington in *The History and Mystery of New Mexico*.

UNDERGROUND BASES

Though there are surface installations, the actual base is located almost two miles beneath Archuleta Mesa on the Jicarilla Apache Indian Reservation near Dulce, New Mexico is an installation classified so secret, its existence is one of the least known in the world. Here is Earth's first and main joint United States Government/alien biogenetics laboratory. Others exist in Colorado, Nevada, and Arizona; however, the one at Dulce is the largest of its kind.

The multi-level facility at Dulce goes down for at least seven known levels, and is reported to have a central HUB which is controlled by base security. The level of security required to access different sections rises as one goes further down the facility. There are over 3000 real-time video cameras throughout the complex at high-security locations (entrances and exits). There are said to be over 100 secret exits near and around Dulce; many around Archuleta Mesa, others to the south around Dulce Lake and even as far east as Lindrith. Deep sections of the complex connect into natural cavern systems.

The Grey Species

Figure 9: Alien Grey

Most of the aliens reside on sub-levels 5, 6, and 7 with alien housing on level 5. The alien species which control the majority of the complex are the Greys, a devious race, now considered an enemy of the New World Order. In the Fifties, the Greys began taking large numbers of humans for experiments. By the Sixties, the rate was speeded up and they began getting careless and self-involved. By the Seventies, their true intentions became very obvious, but the "Special Group" of the Government still kept covering up for them. By the Eighties, the Government realized there was no defense against the Greys. So, programs were enacted to prepare the public for open contact with non-human ET beings.

Perhaps a possible ally to the human race, the Reptoids are an enemy species of the Greys and their relationship is in a constant state of tension. The Greys only known enemy is the Reptilian Race, and there are numerous stories that report that they are on their way to Earth.

A man named Thomas C., famous for stealing the so-called "Dulce Papers[16]", says that there are over 18,000 short "greys" at the Dulce facility. He also has stated how a

---

[16] In 1979, something happened at the base with 66 humans killed and 44 humans escaping. It is suspected that the US attempted unsuccessfully to take over the base by force.

One of the people who in escaped the facility was a CIA agent who, prior to leaving, made some notes, photos, and videotapes, before going into hiding. He has been in hiding ever since, and every six months he contacts each of five people he left copies of the material with. His instructions were that if he missed four successive contacts, the people could do whatever they want with the material. The individuals caring for the packages were non-technical in nature and new very little about the documents.

In December 1987 a Description of these so called "Dulce Papers" was issued, and received by many researchers. The leak is suspected to have come from one of the caretakers of the papers. The Dulce Papers themselves were said to be composed of the following:
•25 black and white photos
•6 minute video tape of Dulce Facility with no dialogue
•set of technical papers pertaining to Facility

The contents included at least the following:

•discussion of copper & molybdenum
•discussion of magnesium & potassium (electrolytes??)
•lots of medical terminology
•discussion of ultraviolet light & gamma rays
•discussion of true purpose of the EBE's
•discussion of usage of cow blood
•discussion of DNA manipulation
•discussion of "almost human beings"
•discussion of "creation of non gender being"
•discussion of DNA manipulation
•discussion of "almost human beings"
•sketches of the photos

colleague of his had come face-to-face with a 6-foot tall Reptoid which had materialized in his house. The Reptoid showed a great interest in research maps of New Mexico and Colorado which were on the wall. The maps were full of colored push-pins and markers to indicate sites of animal mutilations, caverns, locations of high UFO activity, repeated flight paths, abduction sites, ancient ruins, and suspected alien underground bases.

Figure 10: Reptilians are said to be shape shifters.

Some forces in the Government want the public to be aware of what is happening. Other forces (known as The Collaborators or people in the shadows) want to continue making "whatever deals are necessary" for an Elite few to survive the conflicts.

Cloning Humans (by Humans) for Slave Hybrids

There are many stories that the Secret Government has long been cloning humans by a process perfected in the world's largest and most advanced bio-genetic research facility, Los Alamos. According to the stories coming from Los Alamos, these cloned humans are programmed in a manner similar to that used with highly advanced computers. Through this process, the elite humans now have their own disposable slave-race.

Like the alien Greys, the US Government is said to have secretly impregnated human females and then removed the hybrid fetus after a three month time period, before accelerating their growth in laboratories. Biogenetic (DNA Manipulation) programming is then instilled – these hybrids are implanted and controlled at a distance through RF (Radio Frequency) transmissions. Many non-hybrid Humans are also being implanted with these brain transceivers. These implants also work to establish telepathic communication "channels" with the subjects and also act as telemetric brain manipulation devices.

This control network was developed and initiated by the Defense Advanced Research Projects Agency (DARPA)[17]. Two of the procedures were RHIC (Radio-

---

[17] The Defense Advanced Research Projects Agency (DARPA) was established in 1958 to prevent strategic surprise from negatively impacting U.S. national security and create strategic surprise for U.S. adversaries by maintaining the technological superiority of the U.S. military.
To fulfill its mission, the Agency relies on diverse performers to apply multi-disciplinary approaches to both advance knowledge through basic

Hypnotic Intercerebral Control) and EDOM (Electronic Dissolution of Memory). They also developed ELF and EM wave propagation equipment which affect the nerves and can cause nausea, fatigue, irritability, even death. This research into biodynamic relationships within organisms has produced a technology that can change the genetic structure and heal[18].

---

research and create innovative technologies that address current practical problems through applied research. DARPA's scientific investigations span the gamut from laboratory efforts to the creation of full-scale technology demonstrations in the fields of biology, medicine, computer science, chemistry, physics, engineering, mathematics, material sciences, social sciences, neurosciences and more. As the DOD's primary innovation engine, DARPA undertakes projects that are finite in duration but that create lasting revolutionary change.

[18] A current DARPA program is called Neuro Function, Activity, Structure, and Technology (Neuro-FAST)

Military personnel control sophisticated systems, experience extraordinary stress, and are subject to injury of the brain. To address these challenges, DARPA pursues innovative neurotechnology and advanced understanding of the brain using a multidisciplinary approach that combines data processing, mathematical modeling, and novel interfaces. The Neuro Function, Activity, Structure, and Technology (Neuro-FAST) program is part of a broader portfolio of programs within DARPA that support President Obama's brain initiative. The program seeks to enable unprecedented visualization and decoding of brain activity.

For decades, neuroscientists have been limited in their ability to understand the total brain because they have not had the capability to measure all of the critical details of neural circuits. Even today, researchers' understanding of the brain remains fragmented due to gaps in knowledge between brain cells, circuits, and system information processing. Similarly, brain interfaces have the potential to give researchers deep insight into brain function, and to use that knowledge to restore human performance of functional tasks after injury, but current approaches to these devices fall short. They offer no capacity for selective neuron identification combined with neural activity during

Overt and Covert Research

U.S. Energy Secretary John Herrington named the Lawrence Berkeley Laboratory and New Mexico's Los Alamos National Laboratory to house new advanced

---

behavior and can only record small numbers of neurons (hundreds or fewer) en masse. Neuro-FAST aims to address these shortcomings by illuminating new understandings of how the brain operates.

Neuro-FAST builds off of the recently developed CLARITY process, as well as recent discoveries in genetics, optical recordings, and brain-computer interfaces. By combining all four areas, Neuro-FAST seeks to allow researchers to individually identify specific cell types, register the connections between organizations of neurons, and track their firing activity using optical methods in awake, behaving subjects. Neuro-FAST researchers must overcome the dual challenges of achieving single-neuron resolution while simultaneously being able to analyze activity from large numbers of neurons to acquire detailed modeling of the dynamic wiring of neural circuits that cause behavior. Such models would then be coupled with brain activity in real-time to better understand how brain processes work. Neuro-FAST envisions development of novel optical methods to enable the necessary recording.

The data generated by this process would be unlike any previously produced by the neuroscience community and would feed a growing body of knowledge about brain function and form. In addition to fundamental rodent research already underway, Neuro-FAST will expand the processes to non-human primate brains and whole-organ human tissue samples from existing repositories to create a deep understanding across higher-order mammals.

If successful, Neuro-FAST will support pioneering research into brain function over a wide range of spatial and temporal scales to better characterize and mitigate threats to the human brain and facilitate development of brain-in-the loop systems to accelerate and improve functional behaviors.

Neuro-FAST and related DARPA neuroscience efforts are informed by members of an independent Ethical, Legal, and Social Implications (ELSI) panel. Communications with ELSI panelists supplement the oversight provided by institutional review boards that govern human clinical studies and animal use.

genetic research centers as part of a project to decipher the human genome. The genome holds the genetically coded instructions that guide the transformation of a single cell, a fertilized egg, into a biological organism.

"The Human Genome Project may well have the greatest direct impact on humanity of any scientific initiative before us today", said David Shirley, Director of the Berkeley Laboratory.

Covertly, this research has been going on for years at the Dulce bio-genetics labs. Level 6 is hauntingly known by employees as "Nightmare Hall". It holds the genetic labs at Dulce.

Reports from workers who have seen bizarre experimentation are as follows:

"I have seen multi-legged 'humans' that look like half-human/half-octopus. Also reptilian-humans, and furry creatures that have hands like humans and cries like a baby, it mimics human words... also huge mixture of lizard-humans in cages. There are fish, seals, birds and mice that can barely be considered those species. There are several cages (and vats) of winged-humanoids, grotesque bat-like creatures...but 3 1/2 to 7 feet tall. Gargoyle-like beings and Draco-Reptoids."

"Level 7 is worse, row after row of thousands of humans and human mixtures in cold storage. Here too are embryo storage vats of humanoids in various stages of development.

I frequently encountered humans in cages, usually dazed or drugged, but sometimes they cried and begged for help. We were told they were hopelessly insane, and involved in high risk drug tests to cure insanity. We were told to never try to speak to them at all. At the beginning we believed that story.

Finally in 1978 a small group of workers discovered the truth. It began the Dulce Wars". When the truth was evident that humans were being produced from abducted females, impregnated against their will, a secret resistance group formed. This did little though, over time they were assassinated or "died under mysterious circumstances".

As previously stated, there are over 18,000 "aliens" at the Dulce complex. In late 1979, there was a confrontation, primarily over weaponry and the majority of human scientists and military personnel were killed. The facility was closed for a while, but is currently active. Human and animal abductions slowed in the mid-1980s, when the Livermore Berkeley Labs began production of artificial blood for Dulce.

William Cooper states: "A clash occurred where in 66 people, of our people, from the National Recon Group, the DELTA group, which is responsible for security of all alien connected projects, were killed."

The DELTA Group (within Intelligence Support Activity) have been seen with badges which have a black Triangle on a red background. DELTA is the fourth letter of the Greek alphabet. It has the form of a triangle, and figures prominently in certain Masonic Signs. EACH BASE HAS ITS OWN SYMBOL.

The Dulce Base symbol is a triangle with the Greek letter "Tau" (T) within it and then the symbol is inverted, so the triangle points down. The Insignia of "a triangle and 3 lateral lines" has been seen on "Saucer (transport) Craft",

The Tri-Lateral Symbol.

Other symbols mark landing sights and alien craft. Inside the Dulce Complex Security Officers wear jumpsuits, with the Dulce Symbol on the front upper left side.

The standard hand weapon at Dulce is a "Flash Gun", which is good against humans and aliens. The ID card (used in card slots, for the doors and elevators) has the Dulce Symbol above the ID photo. "Government Honchos" use cards with the Great Seal of the U.S. on it, stating the words New World Order in Latin. After the second Level, everyone is weighed in the nude, and then given a uniform. Visitors are given an 'off white' uniform. In front of ALL sensitive areas are scales built under the doorway, by the door control. The person's card must match with the weight and code or the door won't open. Any discrepancy in weight (any change over three pounds) will summon security. No one is allowed to carry anything into or out of sensitive areas.

All supplies are put through a security conveyor system. The Alien Symbol language appears a lot at the Facility. During the construction of the facility (which was done in stages, over many years) the aliens assisted in the design and construction materials. Many of the things assembled by the workers were of a technology they could not understand, yet it would function when fully put together. Example: The elevators have no cables. They are controlled magnetically. The magnetic system is inside the walls. There are no conventional electrical controls. All is controlled by advanced magnetics. That includes a magnetically induced (phosphorescent) illumination system. There are no regular light bulbs. All exits are magnetically controlled. It has been reported that, "If you place a large magnet on an entrance, it will affect an immediate interruption. They will have to come out and reset the system."

Mind Manipulation Experiments

Evidence supports the fact that scientists at the Dulce facility have studied and used mind control implants, Bio-Psi Units, ELF devices capable of mood, sleep and heartbeat control. DARPA is using these technologies to manipulate people. They establish 'The Projects', set priorities, coordinate efforts and guide the many participants in these undertakings.

Related projects are studied at Sandia Base by "The Jason Group" (of 55 scientists). They have secretly harnessed the dark side of technology and hidden the beneficial technology from the public. Other projects take place at the Groom Lake installation in Nevada, also known as Area 51.

ELMINT (Electro-Magnetic Intelligence), Code Empire, Code Eva, Program His (Hybrid Intelligence System), BW/CW, IRIS (Infrared Intruder System), BI-PASS, REP-TILES are said to be some of the research projects under study.

The studies on Level 4 at Dulce include Human-Aura research, as well as all aspects of dreams, hypnosis and telepathy. They know how to manipulate the bioplasmic body of humans. They can lower your heart beat, with deep sleep-inducing delta waves, induce a static shock, and then re-program via a neurological-computer link. They can introduce data and programmed reactions into your mind (information impregnation - the "Dream Library").

We are entering an era of the technologicalization of psychic powers. The development of techniques to enhance man/machine communications, nanotechnology, bio-technological micro-machines, PSI-War, E.D.O.M. (Electronic Dissolution of Memory), R.H.I.C. (Radio-Hypnotic Intra-Cerebral Control) and various forms of behavior control (by chemical agents, ultra-sonics, optical and other forms of EM radiation).

CHAPTER FIVE

WHAT IS KNOWN ABOUT THE DULCE LAB

Since the Dulce Lab, also known as the secret underground base is highly classified, there are no press releases or guide books to the facility, however, there has been a steady stream of data released from various sources. What follows is the best information available at the time of publication.

ADDITIONAL INFORMATION

The following information was given to me while in Dulce and then additional supporting documentation was mailed to me later by a person or persons unknown. I am presenting it just as I received it (author).

In March 2011 I received the following email[19]:

> Lon, I read the letter you posted recently about the Dulce Labs genetics experiments and wanted to share my experiences with your readers. When I was an undergraduate studying genetics in the mid-1970s, I did a 10-month internship at Dulce Labs. My primary duties were on level 1, where I spent almost all of my time. But once a week I accompanied one of the junior researchers to levels 5, 6, and 7 to collect data tapes and other documentation. I never got past the "clear zone" on those levels, but on a couple occasions I heard inhuman shrieks and wailing noises on level 6. I was told that level 6 was a psychiatric facility for especially disturbed patients, and that they were known to have emotional outbursts.
>
> On one occasion while we were waiting for someone to bring out the tapes, I heard part of a message come through the intercom, and the words are burned into my memory.
>
> **VOICE 1:** "CELL 34 COMPROMISED, ENTITY HAS BREACHED CONTAINMENT"

---

[19] The recipient referred to was not the author but rather someone else.

After a pause a second voice came over the speaker:

VOICE 2: "AVAILABLE PERSONAL REPORT TO THE BLUE ZONE FOR C&C. MAXIMUM FORCE AUTHORIZED."

The guard at the desk told me and my colleague that we had to leave immediately. We were rushed back into the elevator before the materials were delivered to us. It was two days before they let us go pick up the tapes, and when we went that time, everything was normal. Nobody ever talked about it. I tried to ask my colleague, the junior researcher who was there at the time, about it, but he said he didn't know what I was talking about, and something in his tone told me I'd better forget about it too.

After I graduated I was interested in returning to Dulce because I was really excited about the potential for genetic science, and Dulce Base had some very advanced equipment and knowledge - better than anything being used anywhere else. But I was told that there weren't any openings. I wondered if I was being blown off because of my curiosity about that event, if I was considered a risk. I tried contacting the junior researcher, but never got a response from him. - MP

The above anecdote was in response to this posted email:

Sir, first off, if you want the full story let me know. But this will explain how Mothman came about. U.S. Energy Secretary John Herrington named the Lawrence Berkeley Laboratory and New Mexico's Los Alamos National Laboratory to house advanced genetic research centers as part of a project to decipher the human genome. The genome holds the genetically coded instructions that guide the transformation of a single cell, a fertilized egg, into a biological organism.

"*The Human Genome Project may well have the greatest direct impact on humanity of any scientific initiative before us today*", said David Shirley, Director of the Berkeley Laboratory.

Covertly, this research has been going on for years at the Dulce bio-genetics labs. Level 6 is hauntingly known by employees as "Nightmare Hall". It holds the genetic labs at Dulce Base.

Reports from workers, who have seen bizarre experimentation, are as follows:

- "I have seen multi-legged 'humans' that look like half-human/half-octopus. Also reptilian-humans, and furry creatures that have hands like humans and cries like a baby, it mimics human words... also huge mixture of lizard-humans in cages. There are fish, seals, birds and mice that can barely be considered those species. There are several cages (and vats) of winged-humanoids, grotesque bat-like creatures...but 3 1/2 to 7 feet tall. Gargoyle-like beings and Draco-Reptoids."

- "Level 7 is worse, row after row of thousands of humans and human mixtures in cold storage. Here too are embryo storage vats of humanoids in various stages of development. I frequently encountered humans in cages, usually dazed or drugged, but sometimes they cried and begged for help. We were told they were hopelessly insane, and involved in high risk drug tests to cure insanity. We were told to never try to speak to them at all. At the beginning we believed that story. Finally in 1978 a small group of workers discovered the truth. It began the Dulce Wars".

When the truth was evident that humans were being produced from abducted females, impregnated against their will, a secret resistance group formed. This did little though. Over time they were assassinated or "died under mysterious circumstances".

The witness also supplied the following information:

- An underground Military Base/Laboratory in Dulce, New Mexico connects with the underground network of tunnels which honeycombs our planet, and the lower levels of this base are allegedly under the control of Inner Earth beings or Aliens. This base is connected to Los Alamos research facilities via an underground "tube-shuttle." (It can be assumed that such a shuttle way would be a straight-line construction. It should then be possible, by using maps and some deduction, to determine the most likely location of this base, especially since the general location is already known.) Beginning in 1947, a road was built near the Dulce Base, under the cover of a lumber company. No lumber was ever hauled, and the road was later destroyed. Navajo Dam is the Dulce

Base's main source of power, though a second source is in El Vado (which is also another entrance). Most of the lakes near Dulce were made via government grants allegedly "for the health and welfare" of the Indians.

Dulce Base - The Central Hub

- 1st Level - contains the garage for Street Maintenance.

- 2nd Level- contains the garage for trains, shuttles, tunnel-boring machines and UFO maintenance.

- 3rd Level - the first 3 levels contain government offices.

- 4th Level - Human Aura Research as well as aspects of Dream Manipulation, Hypnosis, and Telepathy. They can lower your heartbeat with Delta Waves and introduce data and programmed reactions into your mind (for those implanted with brain chips). Most people already are, they just don't know it.

- 5th Level - witnesses have described huge vats with amber liquid with parts of human bodies being stirred inside. Rows and rows of cages holding men, women and children to be used as food. Perhaps thousands.

- 6th Level - privately called "Nightmare Hall." It contains the genetic labs. Here are where the crossbreeding experiments of human/animal are done on fish, seals, birds, and mice that are vastly altered from their original forms. There are multi-armed and multi-legged humans and several cages and vats of humanoid bat-like creatures up to 7 feet tall.

- 7th Level - Row after row of 1,000s of humans in cold storage including children.

It is alleged that Los Alamos and the mountainous regions east and southeast of it in and around the Santa Fe National Forest are the major holding area of earth based extraterrestrial (interterrestrial) beings in North America, although there are a number of smaller habitation locations scattered throughout the underground networks between Dulce and Area 51. 'Dulce Base' is said to hold the second largest repository of extraterrestrials and equipment in North America. None of this information takes into account what resources other nations and governments possess.

All the evidence I have received is anecdotal but, in my opinion, the sources are reliable. You can find more at Dulce Conference Ends / The Dulce Report, What Really Happened in the 1979 Dulce Firefight? and Blue Planet Project - The Dulce Base.

In May 2010, through the MUFON CMS, a Jicarilla Apache tribal police officer recalled an alien encounter he had in Dulce, New Mexico (unedited):

Mid 80's Dulce, NM myself a law enforcement officer w/Jicarilla Apache Police.

Background Police Science/Forensic Western NM Univ., Silver City. Had gone to graveyard shift at midnight w/ another officer and dispatcher. Immediately went to a single female's home with the other shift and was informed that a small being was in her house at the foot of the bed with a box shining a laser like red light at her, the other officers knowing it was there shift change left without further investigation. Making fun mind you.

She was obviously shaken up and I did notice some electrical malfunctions within her home and her animals, dogs and horses were uneasy. Throughout the night I continued to check on her, once in the early morning I was called to her home, her house was dark and as I entered I could hear her down the hall crying for help. I was informed again of visitors with a light in her home and it seemed strangely quiet.

No one to be found in the home or area. In the early morning when the sun comes up when there is light I drove up to the home to make a check I noticed some movement in the brush and trees just west of her home about 15 yards away. I still don't understand what I may have saw, but soon after as I was stepping out of my unit three oval craft in a triangular pattern about the size of a three bedroom home lifted off from behind some juniper trees just 30 yards at the most taking off silently without noise/down drafts, then turn a bright white light and slow went in the direction east towards Chama, NM slowly gain altitude.

My other Officer and Dispatcher was witness to this also. Shortly after I heard on the State Police Frequency from Chama about those UFO.s that were being called in to them. I felt completely helpless as an Officer to help someone who asked for help and was unable to assist and protect her in her time of need. It still bothers me today. S/GJ.

The following are some of the original whistleblowers/witnesses to the activity at the Dulce underground facility.

Thomas Edwin Castello

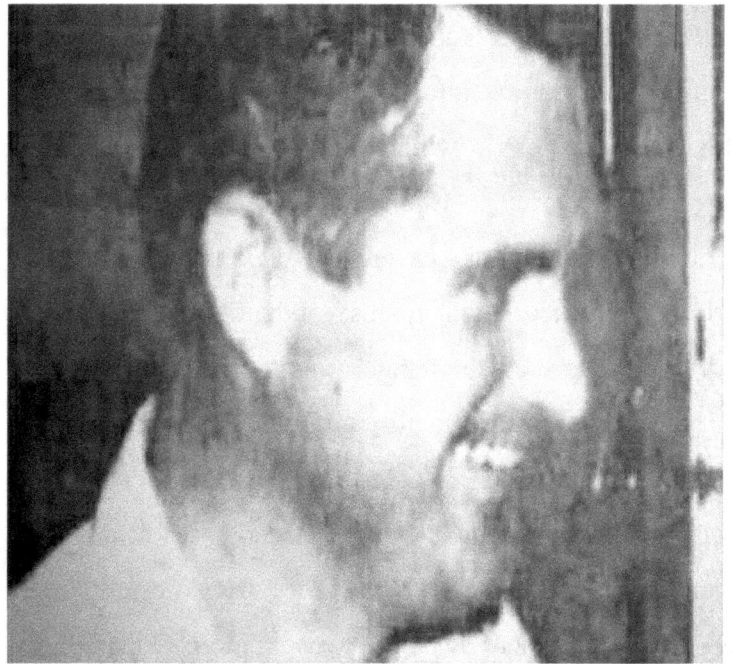

Figure 11: Thomas Castello

Thomas Edwin Castello claimed to be a former security technician, employed by the Rand Corporation, at the Dulce underground facility. However, Castello has only provided stories, nothing solid, and has yet to come forward in person. There is some doubt as to whether he actually exists. He allegedly stole a set of controversial papers called the "Dulce Papers," along with over 30 black and white photos and a video tape.

Castello reported that the Dows [Greys], the Dracos [Reptilians], and the Ciakars are working there hand in hand with over 18,000 short "greys" living the Dulce Facility. A colleague had come face-to-face with a 6-foot tall Reptoid which had materialized in his house. The Reptoid showed an interest in research maps of New Mexico and Colorado which were on the wall. The maps were full of colored push-pins and markers to indicate sites of animal mutilations, caverns, locations of high UFO activity, repeated flight paths, abduction sites, ancient ruins, and suspected alien underground bases.

The multi-level facility at Dulce is reported to have a central HUB which is controlled by base security. The security level goes up as one descends to lower levels. Thomas had an ULTRA-7 clearance. He knew of seven sub-levels, but there may have been more. Most of the aliens supposedly are on levels 5, 6 and 7 with alien housing on level 5. The only sign in English was over the tube shuttle station hallway which read "to Los Alamos."

There appears to be a vast network of tube shuttle connections under the U.S. which extends into a global system of tunnels and sub-cities. Connections go from Dulce to the Page, Arizona facility, then onto an underground base below Area 51 in Nevada. Tube shuttles go to and from Dulce to facilities below Taos, N.M.; Datil, N.M.; Colorado Springs, Colorado; Creed, Colorado; Sandia' then on to Carlsbad, New Mexico.

At the Dulce Base, most signs on doors and hallways are in the alien symbol language and a universal symbol system understood by humans and aliens. Thomas stated that after the second level, everyone is weighed in the nude, and then given a uniform. Visitors are given off-white uniforms; jump suits with a zipper. The weight of the person is put on a computer I.D. card each day. Any change in weight is noted; if over three pounds, a physical exam and X-ray are required.

Scales are located in front of all sensitive areas and are built into the floor near doorways and the door control panels. An individual places his computer I.D. card into the door slot, and then enters a numerical code onto a keypad. The person's weight and code must match the card or the door will not open. Any discrepancy will summon security. No one is allowed to carry anything into sensitive areas. All supplies are put on a conveyor belt and X-rayed. The same method is used in leaving sensitive areas.

All elevators are controlled magnetically; there are no elevator cables. The magnetic system is inside the walls of the elevator shaft, there are no normal electrical controls. Everything is controlled by advanced magnetics, including lighting. There are no regular light bulbs and the tunnels are illuminated by phosphorous units with broad structureless emission bands. Some deep tunnels use a form of phosphorous pentoxide to temporarily illuminate areas. The aliens won't go near these areas for reasons unknown.

Level 1 contains the garage for street maintenance. Level 2 contains the garage for trains, shuttles, tunnel-boring machines and disc maintenance. The studies on Level 4 include human-aura research, as well as all aspects of telepathy, hypnosis, and dreams. Thomas says that they know how to separate the bioplasmic body from the physical body to place an "alien entity" life-force-matrix within a human body after removing the "soul" life-force-matrix of the human.

Level 6 is privately called "Nightmare Hall." It holds the genetic labs, where experiments are done on fish, seals, birds, and mice that are vastly altered from their original form. There are multi-armed and multi-legged humans and several cages (and vats) of humanoid bat-like creatures as tall as 7-feet. The aliens have taught the humans a lot about genetics; things both useful and dangerous.

At Level 7, Thomas encountered humans in cages. Row after row of thousands of humans, human-mixture remains, and embryos of humanoids were kept in cold storage. He says, "I frequently encountered humans in cages, usually dazed or drugged, but sometimes they cried and begged for help. We were told they were hopelessly insane, and involved in high-risk drug tests to cure insanity. We were told to never speak to them at all. At the beginning we believed that story. Finally in 1978 a small group of workers discovered the truth. That began the Dulce wars."

The Grey and Reptoid species are highly analytical and technologically oriented. They have had ancient conflicts with the Nordic humans from other space societies, and may be staging here for a future conflict. Intensely into computing and bio- engineering sciences, they are led to doing reckless experiments without regard for what we consider to be ethical and empathetic conduct toward other living creatures.

Principal government organizations involved in mapping human genetics, the so-called genome projects, are within the Department of Energy (which has a heavy presence on the Nevada Test Site); the National Institute of Health; the National Science Foundation; the Howard Hughes Medical Institute; and, of course, the Dulce Underground Labs which are run by the DOE. Thomas had revealed that the chief of the genetic experiments for Los Alamos and Dulce is Larry Deaven.

According to Thomas, the alien androgynal breeder is capable of parthenogenesis. At Dulce, the common form of reproduction is by polyembryony. Each embryo can, and does divide into 6 to 9 individual "cunne" (pronounced cooney, i.e. siblings). The needed nutriment for the developing cunne is supplied by the "formula," which usually consists of plasma, deoxyhemoglobin, albumin, lysozyme, cation, amniotic fluid and more. The term "genome" is used to describe the totality of the chromosomes unique to a particular organism (or any cell within an organism), as distinct from the genotype, which is the information contained within those chromosomes. The human genes are mapped to specific chromosomal locations. This is an ambitious project that will take years and a lot of computer power to accomplish.

Thomas also says the aliens don't want the land, the gold, the minerals, or water that we possess, nor even the human or animal life. What they do want is magnetic power that surges on and through the Earth. The aliens harvest this magic power in a way unknown to us. Thomas says the aliens recognize this power as more valuable than any other commodity on our globe.

Paul Bennewitz

Figure 12: Paul Bennewitz

Paul Bennewitz, a physicist in Albuquerque and a UFO researcher affiliated with APRO (Aerial Phenomena Research Organization), traveled to Dulce in 1977 to investigate reports of cattle being mutilated on the ranch of Edmound Gomez. He became friends with the local law enforcement official in the area of the Jicarilla Indian Reservation, Gabe Valdez, and the two investigated the mutilations and also some mysterious lights reportedly seen over Archuleta Mesa. Two gentlemen named Howard Burgess and John F. Gille (Jean Francois Gille) also seem to have been involved in these investigations.

Bennewitz along with Dr. Leo Sprinkle then studied the case of Myrna Hansen who said under hypnosis that she had been abducted by the aliens and taken to a secret underground base where they saw the cattle being mutilated and drained of their blood and vats containing human body parts. Implants were placed in the bodies of her and her son and that the aliens could control their minds through these devices.

Bennewitz began filming the strange lights he was seeing over Manzano. He also built a complex electronic surveillance equipment network to receive low-frequency electromagnetic transmissions that he believed came from the alien craft. Bennewitz had several contacts with Air Force Officials that he tried to warn about the threat represented by aliens against the Manzano Weapons Storage Area.

The year after, Bennewitz wrote a computer program that he claimed could translate the alien radio transmissions. He now came to believe that he was intercepting the messages that the aliens were transmitting to mind-control devices such as those that Myrna Hansen claimed had been placed in her and her son.

During this period, 1980 to 1987, Bennewitz was visited by many other UFO researchers, including John Lear and Linda Moulton Howe. In 1987, another abductee named Christa Tilton, added to the tales of underground bases and aliens and vats with human body parts in them.

Bennewitz told Thomas Moore, the famous ufologist, that the alien transmissions he had received indicated that the grays, who he said were responsible for cattle mutilations and the abductions of humans, were building a secret underground base beneath Archuleta Peak on the Jicarilla Indian Reservation near Dulce, New Mexico with the help of the US Government.

When he said in a final burst of paranoia that aliens were coming through the wall of his house to inject him chemicals, it was time to send him to the Hospital. The story says that he has recovered but refuse to deal with the subject of UFOs.

Phil Schneider

Phil Schneider was an engineer who claimed to have discovered the alien base accidentally. Schneider is said to have committed suicide, but others claim he was found with either (1) piano wire, or (2) rubber catheter hose, wrapped around his throat, which indicate that he was murdered, ostensibly to silence him. Some sources say, however, that Schneider both had severe brain damage and was also a paranoid schizophrenic, which makes his stories about Dulce somewhat questionable.

Figure 13: Phil Schneider

"Back in 1954, under the Eisenhower administration, the federal government decided to circumvent the Constitution of the United States and form a treaty with alien entities. It was called the 1954 Greada Treaty, which basically made the agreement that the aliens involved could take a few cows and test their implanting techniques on a few human beings, but that they had to give details about the people involved. Slowly, the aliens altered the bargain until they decided they wouldn't abide by it at all. Back in 1979, this was the reality, and the fire-fight at Dulce occurred quite by accident.

I was involved in building an addition to the deep underground military base at Dulce, which is probably the deepest base. It goes down seven levels and over 2.5 miles deep. At that particular time, we had drilled four distinct holes in the desert, and we were going to link them together and blow out large sections at a time. My job was to go down the holes and check the rock samples, and recommend the explosive to deal with the particular rock. As I was headed down there, we found ourselves amidst a large cavern that was full of outer-space aliens, otherwise known as large Greys. I shot two of them. At that time, there were 30 people down there. About 40 more came down after this started, and all of them got killed. We had surprised a whole underground base of existing aliens. Later, we found out that they had been living on our planet for a long time, perhaps a million years. This could explain a lot of what is behind the theory of ancient astronauts."

CHAPTER SIX

THE DULCE WARS

"*Sixty-six secret service agents, FBI, Black Berets and the like, died in that fire fight. I was there.*" Phil Schneider

Almost twenty years ago this author wrote an action adventure story[20] that contained a battle between aliens and Delta force which, according to my story, resulted in sixty-six soldiers dying. Imagine my surprise when I was made aware of a real battle that allegedly took place in what is called Dulce Base. My story line and what is alleged to have happened at Dulce tracked very closely.

When I was made aware of the so called Dulce Wars, I began to research the situation and asked on my show[21] for any information. Eventually I received the following information about Phil Schneider who was

---

[20] Even Paranoids Have Enemies
[21] Adventure Radio, 1040 AM

alleged to have survived the battle at Dulce. I am repeating the information here just as I received it.

Figure 14: Phil Schneider

Phil Schneider, one of three people to survive the 1979 fire fight between the large Greys, US intelligence and military at the Dulce underground base, was found dead in January of 1996, due to what appears to be an execution style murder. He was found dead in his apartment with a piano wire wrapped around his neck[22]. According to sources, it appeared that he repeatedly suffered torture before he was finally killed. Seven months prior to his death, Schneider did a lecture on the forces he had discovered at Dulce. This brave man's final acts should

---

[22]Certainly an unusual "accident"

not go unnoticed. Below is a synopsis of Phil Schneider. Thank You.

(The following is from a lecture that Phil Schneider gave in the weeks before his death – author)

"It is because of the horrendous structure of the Federal Government that I feel directly imperiled not to tell anybody about this material. However I would like to mention that this talk is going to be broken up into four main topics. Each of these topics will have some bearing on what you people are involved in, whether you are patriots or not."

"I want you to know that these United States are a beautiful place. I have gone to more than 70 countries and cannot remember any country that has the beauty, as well as the magnificence of its people, like these United States."

"To give you an overview of basically what I am, I started off and went through engineering school. Half of my schooling was in that field and I built up a reputation for being a geological engineer, as well as a structural engineer with both military and aerospace applications. I have helped build two main bases in the United States that have some significance as far as what is called the New World Order. The first base is the one at Dulce, New Mexico.

I was involved in 1979 in a fire fight with alien humanoids and I was one of the survivors. I'm probably the only talking survivor you will ever hear. Two other survivors are under close guard. I am the only one left that knows the detailed files of the entire operation. Sixty- six secret service agents, FBI, Black Berets and the like, died in that fire fight. I was there."

"Number one, part of what I am going to tell you is going to be very shocking. Part of what I am going to tell you is probably going to be very unbelievable, though, instead of putting your glasses on, I'm going to ask you to put your ˜scepticals' on. But please, feel free to do your own homework. I know the Freedom of Information Act isn't much to go on, but it's the best we've got. The local law library is a good place to look for Congressional Records. So, if one continues to do their homework, then one can be standing vigilant in regard to their country."

Deep Underground Military Bases

"I love the country I am living in more than I love my life, but I would not be standing before you now, risking my life, if I did not believe it so. The first part of this talk is going to concern deep underground military basses and the black budget.

The Black Budget is a secretive budget that garners 25% of the gross national product of the United States. The Black Budget currently consumes $1.25 trillion per year. At least this amount is used in black programs, like those concerned with deep underground military bases. Presently, there are 129 deep underground military bases in the United States."

"They have been building these 129 bases day and night, unceasingly, since the early 1940's. Some of them were built even earlier than that. These bases are basically large cities underground connected by high-speed magneto-leviton trains that have speeds up to Mach 2. Several books have been written about this activity. Al Bielek has my only copy of one of them.

Richard Souder, a Ph.D. architect, has risked his life by talking about this. He worked with a number of government agencies on deep underground military bases. In around where you live in Idaho, there are 11 of them." "The average depth of these bases is over a mile and they again are basically whole cities underground. They are all between 2.66 and 4.25 cubic miles in size. They have laser drilling machines that can drill a tunnel seven miles long in one day. The Black Projects sidestep the authority of Congress, which as we know is illegal. Right now, the New

World Order is depending on these bases. If I had known at the time I was working on them, that the NWO was involved, I would not have done it. I was lied to rather extensively."

Development of Military Technology, Implied German Interest in Hyperspacial Technology, and More

"Basically, as far as technology is concerned, for every calendar year that transpires, military technology increases about 44.5 years. This is why it is easy to understand that back in 1943 they were able to create, through the use of vacuum tube technology, a ship that could literally disappear from one place and appear in another place. My Father, Otto Oscar Schneider, fought on both sides of the war. He was originally a U-boat captain, was captured and repatriated in the United States. He was involved with different kinds of concerns, such as the A-bomb, the H-bomb and the Philadelphia Experiment. He invented a high-speed camera that took pictures of the first atomic tests at Bikini Island on July 12, 1946. I have original photos of that test; the photos show UFO's fleeing the bomb site at a high rate of speed. Bikini Island at the time was infested with them. Especially under the water and the natives had problems with their animals being mutilated. At that time, General MacArthur felt that the next war would be with aliens from other worlds."

"Anyway, my father laid the groundwork with theoreticians about the Philadelphia experiment, as well as other experiments. What does that have to do with me? Nothing, other than the fact that he was my father. I don't agree with what he did on the other side, but I think that he had a lot of guts coming here. He was hated in Germany. There was a $1 million reward, payable in gold, to anyone who killed him. Obviously, they didn't succeed. Anyway back to our topic - deep underground bases."

The Fire Fight at Dulce Base

"Back in 1954, under the Eisenhower administration, the Federal government decided to circumvent the Constitution of the United States and enter into a treaty with alien entities. It was called the 1954 Greada treaty, which basically made the agreement that the aliens involved could take a few cows and test their implanting techniques on a few human beings, but that they had to give complete details about the people involved to the United States Government. Slowly, the aliens altered the bargain until they decided they wouldn't abide by it at all.

Back in 1979, this was the reality and the fire fight at Dulce occurred quite by accident. I was involved in building an addition to the deep underground military base at Dulce, which is probably the deepest base. It goes down seven levels and over 2.5 miles deep.

At that particular time, we had drilled four distinct holes in the desert and we were going to link them together and blow out large sections at a time. My job was to go down the holes and check the rock samples, and then recommend the explosive to deal with a particular rock. As I was headed down there, we found ourselves amidst a large cavern that was full of outer-space aliens, otherwise known as large Greys. I shot two of them. At that time, there were 30 people down there.

About 40 more came down after this got started and all of them got killed. We had surprised a whole underground base of existing aliens. Later, we found out that they had been living on our planet for a long time, perhaps a million years. This could explain a lot of what is behind the theory of ancient astronauts."

"Anyway I got shot in the chest with one of their weapons, which was a box on their body that blew a hole in me and gave me a nasty dose of cobalt radiation. I have had cancer because of that."

"I didn't get really interested in UFO technology until I started work at Area 51, north of Las Vegas. After about two years recuperating after the 1979 incident, I went back to work for Morrison and Knudson, EG&G and other companies. At Area 51, they were testing all kinds of spacecraft. How many people here are familiar with Bob Lazar's story? He was a physicist working at Area 51 trying to decipher the propulsion factor in some of these craft".

Schneider's Worries About Government Factions, Railroad Cars and Shackle Contracts

"Now, I am very worried about the activity of the Federal Government. They have lied to the public stonewalled senators and have refused to tell the truth in regard to alien matters. I can go on and on. I can tell you that I am rather disgruntled.

Recently, I knew someone who lived near where I live in Portland, Oregon. He worked at Gunderson Steel Fabrication, where they make railroad cars. Now, I knew this fellow for the best part of 30 years and he was a quiet type. He came in to see me on it, one day, excited, he told me "they're building prisoner cars.'

He was nervous. Gunderson he said had a contract with the Federal Government to build 107,200 full length railroad cars, each with 143 pairs of shackles. There are 11 sub-contractors in this giant project. Supposedly, Gunderson got over 2 billion dollars for the contract. Bethlehem Steel and other steel outfits are involved. He showed me one of the cars in the rail yards in North Portland.

He was right. If you multiply 107,200 times 143 times 11, you come up with about 15,000,000. This is probably the number of people who disagree with the Federal Government. No more can you vote these people out of office. Our present structure of government is "technocracy"- not democracy, it is a form of feudalism. It has nothing to do with the republic of the United States. These people are godless and have legislated out prayer in public schools. You can get fined up to $100.000 and two years in prison for praying in school. I believe we can do better, also believe that the Federal Government is running the gambit of enslaving the people of the United States. I am not a very good speaker, but I'll keep shooting my mouth off until somebody puts a bullet in me, because it's worth it to talk to a group like this about these atrocities".

Americas Black Program Contractors

"There are other problems. I have some interesting 1993 figures. There are 29 prototype stealth aircraft presently. The budget from the US Congress five-year plan for these is $245.6 million.

You couldn't buy the spare parts for these black programs for that amount. So, we've been lied to. The black budget is roughly $1.3 trillion every two years. A trillion is a thousand billion. A trillion dollars weighs 11 tons. The US Congress never sees the books involved with this clandestine pot of gold. Contractors of stealth programs: EG&G, Westinghouse, McDonnell Douglas, Morrison-Knudson, Wackenhut Security Systems, Boeing Aerospace, Lorimar Aerospace, Aerospacial in France, Mitsubishi Industries, Ryder Trucks, Bechtel, I G Farben, plus a host of hundreds more. Is this what we are supposed to be living up to as a freedom-loving people? I don't believe so."

Star Wars and Apparent Alien Threat

"Still, 68% of the military budget is directly or indirectly affected by the black budget. Star Wars relies heavily upon stealth weaponry. By the way, none of the stealth program would have been available if we had not taken apart crashed alien disks. None - of it. Some of you might ask what the "space shuttle" is "shuttling." Large ingots of special metals that are milled in space and cannot be produced on the surface of the earth. They need the near vacuum of outer space to produce them. We are not even being told anything close to the truth. I believe our government officials have sold us down the drain lock, stock and barrel.

Up until several weeks ago, I was employed by the US government with a Ryolite-38 clearance factor - one of the highest in the world. I believe the Star Wars program is there to solely to act as a buffer to prevent an alien attack - It has nothing to do with the "cold war", which was only a toy to garner money from all the people - for what? The whole lie was planned and executed for the last 75 years."

Stealth Aircraft Technology Use by US Agencies and the United Nations

"Here's another piece of information for you folks. The Drug Enforcement Administration and the ATF rely on stealth tactical weaponry for as much as 40% of their operations budget. This is in 1993; the figures have gone up considerably since. The United Nations used American stealth aircraft for over 20% of its collective world-wide operations from 1990 to 1992, according to the Centre for Strategic Studies and UN Report 3092.11

The Guardians of Stealth and Delta Force Origins of the Bosnia Conflict

"The guardians of Stealth: There are at least three distinct classifications of police that guard our most well-kept secrets.

- Number one, the Military Joint Tactical Force (MJTF), sometimes called the Delta Force or Black Berets, is a multi-national tactical force primarily used to guard the various stealth aircraft worldwide. By the way, there were 172 stealth aircraft built. Ten crashed, so there were at last count about 162. Bill Clinton signed them away about six weeks ago to the United Nations. There have been indications that the Delta Force was sent over to Bosnia during the last days of the Bush administration as a covert sniper force and that they started taking pot shots at each side of the controversy, in order to actually start the Bosnia conflict that would be used by succeeding administrations for political purposes."

Thoughts on the Bombings in the United States

"I was hired not too long ago to do a report on the World Trade Centre bombing. I was hired because the 90 some - odd varieties of chemical explosives. I looked at the pictures taken right after the blast. The concrete was puddled and melted. The steel and the rebar were extruded up to six feet longer than its original length. There is only one weapon that can do that - a small nuclear weapon. That's a construction-type device. Obviously, when they say that it was a nitrate explosive that did the damage, they're lying 100% folks. The people that they have in custody probably didn't do the crime. As a matter of fact, I have reason to believe that the same group held in custody did do other crimes, such as killing a Jewish rabbi in New York. However, I want to further that with the last explosion in Oklahoma City, they are saying that it was a nitrate or fertilizer bomb that did it."

"First they came out and said it was a 1,000 pound fertilizer bomb. Then it was 1,500. Then 2,000 pounds. Now it's 20,000. You can't put 20,000 pounds of fertilizer in a Ryder Truck. Now, I've never mixed explosives, per se. I know the chemical structure and application of construction explosives. My reputation was based on it. I helped hollow out more than 13 deep underground military bases in the United States.

I worked on the Malta project, in West Germany, in Spain and in Italy. I can tell you from experience that a nitrate explosion would not have shattered the windows of the federal building in Oklahoma City.

It would have killed a few people and knocked part of the facing off the building, but it would never have done that kind of damage. I believe that I have been lied to and I am not taking it any longer, so I'm telling you that you've been lied to."

The Truth Behind the Republican Contract with America

"I don't perceive at this time that we have too much more than six months of life left in this country, at the present. We are the laughing stock of the world, because we are being hoodwinked by so many evil people that are running this country. I think we can do better. I think the people over 45 are seriously worried about their future. I'm going to run some scary scenarios by you. The Contract with America. It contains the same terminology that Adolph Hitler used to subvert Germany in 1931. I believe that we can do better. The Contract with America is a last ditch effort by our federal government to tear away the Constitution and the Bill of Rights."

Some Statistics on the Black Helicopter Presence

"The black helicopters. There are over 64,000 black helicopters in the United States. For every hour that goes by, there is one more being built. Is this the proper use of our money? What does the federal government need 64,000 tactical helicopters for, if they are not trying to enslave us? I doubt if the entire military needs 64,000 worldwide. I doubt if the entire world needs that many. There are 157 F-117A stealth aircraft loaded with LIDAR and computer-enhanced imaging radar.

They can see you walking from room to room when they fly over your house. They see objects in the house from the air with a variation limit of 1 inch to 30,000 miles. That's how accurate it is. Now, I worked in the federal government for a long time and I know exactly how they handle their business."

Government Earthquake Device, AIDS as a Bioweapon Based on Alien Excretions.

"The federal government has now invented an earthquake device. I am a geologist and I know what I am talking about. With the Kobe earthquake in Japan, there was no pulse-wave as in a normal earthquake. None. In 1989, there was an earthquake in San Francisco. There was no pulse-wave with that one either. It is a Tesla device that is being used for evil purposes. The black budget programs have subverted science as we know it. Look at AIDS, invented by the National Ordinance Laboratory in Chicago, Illinois in 1972. It was a biological weapon to be used against the people of the United States. The reason that I know that is that I have seen the documentation by the Office of Strategic Services, which is by the way still in operation to this day, through the CDC in Atlanta.

They used the glandular excretions of animals, humans and alien humanoids to create the virus. These alien humanoids that the government is hobnobbing with are the worst news. There is absolutely no defense against their germs -none. They are a biological weapon of terrible consequence. Every alien on the planet needs to be isolated."

"Saddam Hussein killed 3.5 million Kurdish people with a similar biological weapon. Do we, the people of this planet, deserve this? No, we don't, but we are not doing anything about it. Every moment we waste, we are doing other people on the planet a disservice."

"Right now I am dying of cancer that I contracted because of my work for the federal government. I might live six months. I might not. I will tell you one thing. If I keep speaking out like I am, maybe God will give me the life to talk my head off. Eleven of my best friends in the last 22 years have been murdered. Eight of the murders were called "suicides."

Before I went to talk in Las Vegas, I drove a friend down to Joshua Tree, near 29 Palms. I drove into the mountains in order to get to Needles, California and was followed by two government E-350 vans with G-14 plates, each with a couple of occupants, one of which had an Uzi. I knew exactly who they were. I have spoken 19 times and have probably reached 45,000 people. Well, I got ahead of them and came to a stop in the middle of the road. They both went on either side of me and plummeted into a ravine. Is this what it is going to take? I cut up my security card and sent it back to the government and told them if I was threatened, I have been, that I was going to upload

140,000 pages of documentation to the Internet about government structure and the whole plan. I have already begun that task. Thank you very much."

Phil Schneider May 1995

Phil Schneider never got the chance to do anything about the dangers that he discussed. He was dead seven months after this lecture.

CHAPTER SEVEN

A MYSTERIOUS DEATH

There are many who feel that the death of Phil Schneider is directly related to his knowledge of the Dulce Base. He had been a problem for the Shadow Rulers as he was lecturing around the country regarding some of the incidents and mysteries of Dulce. Whether you believe he was telling the truth or nor, this would hardly be grounds for murder – unless perhaps he was getting too close to certain truths that the "powers that be" did not want revealed.

Phil Schneider died – one of many UFO related researchers to die over the years of unusual causes or in unusual circumstances. The authorities wrote it off as a suicide, but what does the evidence say?

The following information was publicized by his ex-wife. Whether the reader believes that Phil Schneider committed suicide or was murdered, It does make interesting reading.

Testimony of Phil's Ex-Wife, Cynthia Schneider Drayer Concerning Phil Schneider and His Death

A Small Introduction
Intro by Cynthia Drayer

My name is Cynthia Drayer, I live in Portland, Oregon, and I am the ex-wife of Philip Schneider. Philip and I met in 1986, were married in Carson City, Nevada, and had a daughter, Marie, in 1987. We were divorced in 1990 and lived in separate residences. Philip lived in an apartment complex in Wilsonville, Oregon. On 1/17/1996 I received a call that Philip was dead in his apartment and apparently had died up to a week before his body was discovered. At the time of the removal of his body, his cause of death was by a stroke. When I went to the funeral home I had feelings of discomfort about his death. I asked to view the body, but due to decomposition, the funeral director suggested otherwise. I wanted to be sure in my own mind that Philip had not died under "unnatural causes". For the last two years of his life, Philip had been on the "lecture tour" throughout the United States, talking out about government cover-ups.

You name it, he was talking about it: Aliens (treaties and abductions), UFO's, the One World Government, Black Budgets, Underground Mountain Bases, CIA involvement in civilian murders and drugs, Stealth technology, the Philadelphia Experiment, Operation Crossroads (Bikini Island A-bomb experiments), Dulce Fire Fight, the Oklahoma bombing, the World Trade Center bombing, missing children, Gunderson Freight Cars, the opening of concentration camps and Marshal Law/UN involvement, man-made viruses and earthquakes, etc. etc.

A day later, I received a call from the Clackamas County Detectives, that the funeral director had found "something" around Philip's neck. An autopsy was performed at the Multnomah County Medical Examiner's Office (in Portland, Oregon) by Dr. Gunson, and she determined that Philip had committed suicide by wrapping a rubber catheter hose three times around his neck, and half-knotting it in front. There are several reasons why I believe that Philip did not commit suicide, but was murdered:

1. There was no suicide note.
2. Philip always told his friends and relatives, that if he ever "committed suicide" you would know that he had been murdered.

3. From a number of sources, including his taped lectures (video and audio), and statements to his friends, and the borrowing of a 9mm gun, Philip felt that he and his family were being threatened and were in danger because of his lectures.
4. All of his lecture materials, alien metals, higher math books, photographs of UFO's coming out of the Operation Crossroads A-Bomb, notes for his book on the alien agenda, were missing. (Everything else in the apartment was still there, including gold coins, wallet with hundreds of dollars, jewelry, mineral specimens, etc.)
5. No coroner ever came out to his apartment after his body was found (against Oregon Law) - and a police investigation never took under consideration that items were missing from his apartment - it was considered a suicide, plain and simple
6. The medical examiner took blood and urine samples at the autopsy but REFUSED to analyze them, saying that the county would not "waste their money on a suicide". Although I was assured that the samples would be kept for 12 months, when I asked for these samples to be sent to an independent lab 11 months later they were "missing" and presumed "destroyed".

7. Philip had missing fingers on his left hand, and limited motion in his shoulders. I believe that it was physically impossible for Philip to have held the rubber hose in his left hand with missing fingers and then wrap the hose three times with shoulders that had limited motion. In order to end up where his body was, he had to sit on the edge of his bed, wrap the hose around his neck, slowly and painfully strangle to death, and fallen head first into a wheel chair.
8. Philip was an expert in chemicals and his own medical needs. He had multiple pills at hand that could have ended his life quickly and painlessly. He also had a 9mm gun that he had borrowed to protect himself. Why (did he) strangle himself in such an unusual manner?
9. Philip was very religious, and did not believe in suicide. He had intense chronic pain all of the time I knew him. At the time of his death, he was on disability, had a housekeeper, and had cancer. The operation to help him with his back pain did not alleviate the pain and he had brittle bone syndrome (osteoporosis). He struggled every day, not to die, but to live.

He felt that these lectures he gave was making a difference, and was looking forward to giving more. In fact he was scheduled for another lecture tour that started 1/16/96 in Tampa, Florida. He had just found a friend who was going to help him write a book about the New World Order, and he was enjoying his time with his daughter.

10. Philip was undergoing "injections" of "Beta Serone" every week in an experiment to stop his multiple sclerosis. After his death I contacted the only agency that conducted these experiments to obtain his medical record (OHSU). They had never heard of him, and he was not a part of their experiments. This would suggest That people unknown were injecting him on a weekly basis with an unknown substance. He often times called me after these "shots" to tell me that he was too sick for his daughter to come and visit. I believe that the shots that Philip thought were being given to him to help him back to health, were actually being given to him to make him sick.

11. Philip was seen with an "unknown blonde haired woman" for several months before his death. Several times this same individual was seen or talked about and her mysterious presence only leads one to wonder if she had anything to do with his "suicide".

12. Several people with psychic abilities have indicated that Philip did not commit suicide, but was murdered (some say by 5 people: 4 men and 1 woman, 4 directly and one by taking out a "contract".

It is perhaps important to know WHY Philip began lecturing.

- Firstly: His background was as a Structural Engineer. He was an expert on explosives and their effects on geologic structures. He worked under two social security numbers. Most of his early work in underground mountain bases with Morrison-Knudsen was done using the wrong social security number. I was later able to prove that he had two numbers through the social security office when I applied for his daughter's death benefits. He worked for the Army Corps of Engineers and U.S. Navy with the same wrong number. Only after he obtained SSI in 1981 did his "real" number come into play. He always told me that he had a Rhyolitic Clearance and that his father had a Cosmic Clearance from his work with NATO. And that is the second reason why Philip began lecturing.
- Secondly: On top of his first-hand knowledge about underground mountain bases and government black

budgets, and the alien agendas (he was one of the survivors of the Dulce Fire Fight with aliens in New Mexico) his father was also involved in government black projects.

When Philip's father, Captain Oscar Schneider, Medical Doctor, United States Navy, died in 1993, Philip discovered documents and photographs in his father's basement which proved that Oscar had been involved in both the Philadelphia Experiment and Operation Crossroads. Philip now had letters written in the 1940's and 1950's showing that Oscar helped to isolate the crewmembers of the Philadelphia Experiment and that Oscar later autopsied them as they died. He also had photographs of UFO's fleeing through mushroom clouds after the A-bomb was dropped above the lagoon at Bikini Atoll. This was "Operation Crossroads" and Oscar was involved in medical examinations of the animals and humans exposed to radiation after the bomb was dropped.

- Thirdly: I believe the main reason why Philip began to lecture was due to the "murder" of his friend Ron Rummel. Ron was found in a park in Portland in Sept. 1993. The police believed that he had committed suicide by shooting himself in the mouth. However, if you read the detectives report, there is blow-back blood on Ron's hand, but NO BLOW-BACK BLOOD ON THE GUN. The only way this could happen is if Ron had wiped the gun off AFTER he had shot himself in the mouth. Ron, Philip, and 5 other people had been collaborating on a little magazine called "The Alien Digest". It was starting to get a fairly wide circulation, when Ron was found in the park. Philip felt that his friend had been murdered, and decided that it was time to get everything out into the open, so he began "spilling the beans", and ripped up his security clearance card. Pufori, through Jeroen Wierda, is one of several agencies and individuals that have taken up the call for justice in Philip's death.

My hopes are:
1. That Philip's death certificate will eventually be amended with the true cause of his death: murder.
2. That the world will come to know the truth about aliens, UFO's, the government cover-ups, black budgets, etc. and how they are affecting us.

3. That assets that belong to his only heir, Marie, can be located and turned over to her.
4. That Philip's true work quarters can be proven by people coming forward with information about knowing him before 1981 and that his daughter can eventually obtain the death benefits she deserves.
5. That no more "murders by suicide" ever occur to another individual.

Please look over the information contained in this website. The "truth is out there" and it is here.

Sincerely, Cynthia Schneider Drayer

The material submitted by Cynthia Drayer is certainly interesting and if true, could well support a finding of murder. The problem is in almost every situation there are three sides to any argument – your side, their side and the facts. Which have we been given in this situation?

Was Schneider murdered because he talked about Dulce or was he killed for some other reason?

PART TWO

STRANGE CREATURES

CHAPTER EIGHT
CREATURES OF THE NIGHT

As if aliens and secret underground alien bases are not enough, there are also spectral creatures of the night that are said to roam the countryside in the four corners region. Among these creatures are skin walkers.

In some Native American legends, a skin-walker is a person with the supernatural ability to turn into any animal he or she desires. To be able to transform, legend sometimes requires that the skin-walker wears a pelt of the animal. In most cases, this pelt is not used in modern times because it is an obvious sign of them being skin-walkers.

Similar lore can be found in cultures throughout the world and is often referred to as shapeshifting by anthropologists. It should also be added that shapeshifting is among the powers attributed to some of the alien species believed to inhabit the base at Dulce.

Navajo skin walker: the yee naaldlooshi

Possibly the best documented skin walker beliefs are those relating to the Navajo yee naaldlooshii (literally "with it, he goes on all fours" in the Navajo language). A yee naaldlooshii is one of several varieties of Navajo witch (specifically an 'ánti'įhnii or practitioner of the Witchery Way, as opposed to a user of curse-objects ('adagąsh) or a practitioner of Frenzy Way ('azhįtee)).

Technically, the term refers to an 'ánt'įįhnii who is using his (rarely her) powers to travel in animal form. In some versions, men or women who have attained the highest level of priesthood are called clizyati, "pure evil", when they commit the act of killing a close blood relative (sister, brother, mother, father), incest, or necrophilia. This act is said to destroy their humanity and allow them to fully immerse themselves in the teachings of the Witchery Way.

The 'ánt'įįhnii are human beings who have gained supernatural power by breaking a cultural taboo. Specifically, a person is said to gain the power to become a yee naaldlooshii upon initiation into the Witchery Way. This is done especially via the Navajo equivalent of the

'Black Mass', a perverted "sing" (Navajo ceremonial) used to curse instead of to heal. Both men and women can become 'ánt'įįhnii and therefore possibly skin walkers, but men are far more numerous. It is generally thought that only childless women can become witches. Not every witch is a skin walker, but every skin walker is a witch.

Although a skin walker is most frequently seen as a coyote, wolf, fox, eagle, owl, or crow the yee naaldlooshii is said to have the power to assume the form of any animal they choose, a decision based on what specific abilities are needed. For example, Witches may use a bird form for expedient travel in pursuit, escape, or otherwise. Some Navajo also believe that skin walkers have the ability to steal the face of a person. The Navajo believe that if you ever lock eyes with a skin walker, they can absorb themselves into your body. Alternately, some Navajos believe that if you make eye contact with a skin walker, your body will freeze up due to the fear of them and the skin walker will use that fear to gain power and energy.

A skin walker is usually described as hairy, except for an animal skin. Some Navajos describe them as a perfect version of the animal in question. The skin may just be a mask, like those which are the only garment worn in the witches' sing, which is the opposite of the good sing.

Because animal skins are used primarily by skin walkers, the pelt of animals such as bears, coyotes, wolves, and cougars are considered taboo. Sheepskin and buckskin are probably two of the few hides used by Navajos; the others are not used for ceremonial purposes.

Often, Navajo people will tell of their encounter with a skin walker, though many hesitate to reveal the story to non-Navajos, or to talk of such things at night. Sometimes the skin walker will try to break into the house and attack the people inside, and will often bang on the walls of the house, knock on the windows, and climb onto the roofs. Sometimes, a strange, animal-like figure is seen standing outside the window, peering in. Other times, a skin walker may attack a vehicle and cause a car accident.

The skin walkers are described as being fast, agile, and impossible to catch. Though some attempts have been made to shoot or kill one, they are not usually successful. Sometimes a skin walker will be tracked down, only to lead to the house of someone known to the tracker. As in European werewolf lore, sometimes a wounded skin walker will escape, only to have someone turn up later with a similar wound which reveals them to be the witch.

It is said that if a Navajo was to know the person behind the skin walker they had to pronounce the full name, and about three days later that person would either get sick or die for the wrong that they have committed.

Legend has it skin walkers can have the power to read human thoughts. They also possess the ability to make any human or animal noise they choose. A skin walker may use the voice of a relative or the cry of an infant to lure victims out of the safety of their homes; the skin walkers cannot enter a home without invitation.

The yee naaldlooshi are distinguishable in human form because their eyes glow like an animal's. In animal form they can be spotted by moving stiffly and unnaturally, and their eyes do not glow like an animal's.

Skin walkers use charms to instill fear and control in their victims. Such charms include human bone beads launched by blowguns, which embed themselves beneath the surface of the skin without leaving a mark and human bone dust which can cause paralysis and heart failure. Skin walkers have been known to find traces of their victim's hair, wrap it around a pot shard, and place it into a tarantula hole. Even live rattlesnakes are known to be used as charms by the skin walker. A skin walker can use anything of personal belongs and use in ceremonial rituals against the person they are doing evil against.

Skin-walkers use a powder called corpse dust, also known as corpse poison, corpse powder, and án't'i, to poison victims. Corpse dust is composed of ground infant bones, preferably twin infants, and bones from the fingertips and back of the skull. The yee naaldlooshi blow it into the faces of their victims, or down the chimney of the victims' home. Soon after the victim breathes the dust the tongue starts to swell and blacken, and they go into convulsions and die.

TOTEMS AND MEDICINE MEN

The Navajo people have a very strong emotional bond with the Earth and the plant and animal kingdoms that are so much a part of their everyday lives.[citation needed] Certain animals are more sacred to some individuals, families and tribes. These animals could be said to bless, heal or guide the people and become totem animals.

Totem animals are honored with their likeness in the dress, dance, music and artwork of the people. The traits and characteristics of the totem animals could be gifted to the people who developed a deep friendship with the spirits of these helpful creatures. Some individuals developed such a deep connection with nature and her magic that they could talk with the plants and animals and bring knowledge of medicine and other healing arts to their tribes. These few adepts became medicine men, healers, or wise ones.

Medicine men were known to be able to travel to other states of being. It was through the gifts of their totem animals that this travel was made. They were often seen wearing the skin of the animal that granted them this power and would sometimes be seen in animal form.

Often ancestors and heroes would appear as animals important or sacred to the family or tribe, or as an animal the individual was known for. People especially reported seeing these strangely human animals when receiving good fortune or divine messages. Some would hear the animals speak to them, act as a human would or witness impossible colors or breeds that do not exist.

A medicine man should never be confused with a practitioner of the witchery or frenzy way. In the Navajo culture there is a clear distinction between a witch and a medicine man. Medicine men practice healing arts, blessings and the removal of curses. Any Navajo practicing the witchery way is evil; the intent of such practice is purely to harm others of their own tribe and rarely people outside of it.

These stories were related by a medicine man during my search for Bigfoot. They are being laid out here just as they were recorded.

Being a Native American you will find many of the common beliefs about Bigfoot or Sasquatch. In most of the languages it translates to the forest people or Mountain People. In the culture they are looked at as a spirit person but they are considered a person in their own right. Now Being a Ranger in the Dulce NM area for the Jicarilla Apache Reservation for many years I had heard stories when I would be up there Visiting before I had moved there. And well as you know some things are just a story of a story of someone who had heard something.

Well I had a few encounters to make me realize that there is something out there in the woods. Let me tell you about my first encounter with one of them. Myself and another medicine man had gone up into the mountain area that many have heard called Archuleta mesa. (Ufo Base Mountain) and the canyon that is a long winding road going up there is Called "Big Foot Canyon" by the locals that are there and many have had encounters with them in that area.

There is the Navajo river that runs down through the bottom of the Canyon area there and many have seen it down in that area. This time we had driven way up the winding canyon all the way to the top area that reaches a peak and overlooks the New Mexico and Colorado border and from the top there you can see into Colorado into what is the Ute reservation that borders the Jicarilla reservation.

Well we stopped up there to take a break and just get out and walk around and take in the beauty of the canyon. We weren't up there for maybe about 15 minutes and we heard the most Bone chilling noise I can say I have ever heard in the mountain area. The only way to describe it was something VERY larges screaming out loud and it sounded similar to a Howler monkey and a Peacock type of a sound mixed together. In all my years of being up in the mountain I had never heard anything like it. It made the hair on my arms stand straight up and we looked at each other and were both baffled by the sound.

My son was with me and he was about 9 years old at the time and got really scared and said "Dad what is that? I'm scared!" so of course I'm joking around with my son and say..... Well son we are in big foot canyon......It a Bigfoot!! Well he got really scared and wanted to leave so I told him don't worry I have my Rifle and nothing is going to get us. Well we sat there and heard it screaming off and on for about 10 minutes. I wish I had a recorder or my camera in case I saw it. Well I didn't think too much more about it until I head down the canyon what almost sounded like wood being chopped like a big log whacking a tree or something like that and then some more screaming from it.

Well at this time we decided to go down the mountain and make a day of it. Later on that week we went into Albuquerque to visit my parents and we were watching the television and I tuned into some show on Sasquatch and they were talking about sounds that were recorded up in Washington state....... well when they played them it really made the hair stand up on my neck, this was almost an identical sound!! I told my son to listen and tell me what it sounded like and even he said....."That's what we heard up in Bigfoot canyon"

During the past several months, I have accorded some attention to several unexplained livestock attacks and cryptid sightings on the Dine Navajo lands in the Four Corners region...in particular, those areas in northwest New Mexico. Many of these attacks were, most likely, the result of Bigfoot-type hominids that are regularly seen in this area. Other attacks have a more bizarre angle, especially when the tracks of the perpetrator are of an unfamiliar genus and / or suddenly end in mid-stride as well as animal carcasses drained of blood and not fed upon.

The Archuleta Mesa area near Dulce, New Mexico has long been rumored to hold a joint government-alien biogenetic laboratory designed to carry out bizarre experiments on humans and animals. It has also been said that the lower levels of this underground system stretches between Dulce and Los Alamos some 90 miles to the south-east. Because of the proximity of these facilities to the Dine Navajo lands, is it possible that these attacks are of unknown experimental beings that have either escaped from the facility or have been released in order to be scientifically monitored. It may seem to be a far-fetched hypothesis...unless, of course, you are the victim of the attacks and have no idea of what you're dealing with.

During one of my interviews I talked to an EMT who worked the night shift. I have long thought that those who worked the night shift had the most interesting of jobs since anything weird usually took place at night. During the interview, she talked about strange looking creatures being seen alongside of the roads within the reservation that literally defied description. On several occasions she had seen man-sized reptilian looked creatures walking on two legs.

I asked if she had reported her sightings and she told me emphatically that if you wanted to keep your job you did not discuss such things at work, but it was an open secret that strange creatures roamed the reservation at night.

CHAPTER NINE

OTHER TUNNELS

It is interesting to note how much in the way of fringe writings are sent to me as a result of the type of books that I write. I made mention at a talk about how the Dulce Base was said to be connected to a vast underground system of tunnels that is said to crisscross the nation. Shortly I received the following in an email. It came from something called CONTACT: THE PHOENIX PROJECT[23], June 20, 1995:

"I happened to mention that I had heard, very early after the Oklahoma City bombing, some mention of there being an 18-story underground associated with that

---

[23] I am not really sure what Contact is, but it must have a tremendous amount of information about these mysterious tunnels.

building, including five floors of underground parking garage space. This tantalizing bit of news came about because some network TV interviewer was discussing the bomb pattern with, I think, the building's original designer or architect.

"But I never heard it mentioned again, in all the days of further reporting, as the enormous magnitude of that tragedy continued to unfold, amidst spin doctoring of the most dazzling intensity (that is, anti-militia and anti-patriot 'spin-doctoring'. - Branton)

"As happens in such cases of instant news sanitation, one begins to question if one EVER REALLY heard what one was SURE of just a week or so earlier. After all, you would think such information couldn't easily be hidden so well.

"So, in that 5/30/95 Front Page editorial I asked if anyone else out there had heard about this interesting and apparently 'neglected' feature of the Oklahoma City federal building. After all, longtime CONTACT readers are well aware of all the diabolical, tunnel-interconnected, secret underground facilities around the country. Thus, even the mere possibility of a major UNDERGROUND aspect to the structure beings a whole new provocative array of dimensions into this already bizarre picture called the 'official' Oklahoma City blast story. For instance, the 'rumors' about serious Fed-incriminating Waco evidence being stored at that Oklahoma City site take on new life if an underground connection is genuine (for instance, there were reports that some agents IGNORED wounded children and employees among the ruins and went instead straight into the rubble to 'rescue' the boxes of secret implicating documents deeper within the building. Or did they remove these documents only to be destroyed at a later time, so that 'they' could claim that all of this 'evidence' had been destroyed in the blast? - Branton).

"On 6/7/95 we received an interesting, excited telephone call at the CONTACT offices from someone who had read my editorial and could confirm having heard EARLY news reports which were not only similar to what I had heard, but made what I heard sound like last week's used coffee grounds. Rick Martin took the call and, after hearing the news, asked this person to take a deep, calming breath and then put their thoughts down on paper.

"Let me quote from that letter, received at the CONTACT offices on 6/15/95. This is from E.B.W., writing from the Pacific Northwest State of Washington.

"I watched the Oklahoma bombing right after it happened. I had the TV on and all of a sudden it switched to this scene where a bombing had just taken place. At first, I did not pay much attention; I was busy doing something else. I would listen in every once in a while. The anchorwoman, or reporter, from the local TV station, was running around, babbling excitedly. At least once, that I remember, all people were asked to leave the scene and it showed everybody running like mad. They had found additional bombs, or bomb, and the detonation squad was called in to defuse it.

"During all this commotion, running and reporting, the lady reporter kept talking about the underground tunnels, which had been blown open. She kept referring to the huge underground tunnels and there may be people trapped in there. I heard her refer to the underground tunnels at least about 6 to 7 times during the period I watched. I'm not quite sure how long that was. Maybe 1 to 2 hours.

"A lady friend of mine called me and wanted to know if I had seen the fireman on the scene, who went in front of the camera, totally freaked, wide-eyed and scared, who talked about huge underground tunnels, where enormous supplies of arms were stored. He said he saw missiles, tanks, ETC., ETC. I don't remember what else he saw. But he was totally freaked out. He looked like he had seen a ghost. Hope this helps.

P.S. Please don't use my name. I will try to get my friend to write down what she knows."

An 18-level underground base? CIA involvement? A huge military arsenal? Unless I'm mistaken, could this be one of the New World Order underground bases mentioned by Phil Schneider? If so, then if or when an attempted United Nations crack-down on American Patriots, and/or a possible European New World Order invasion of American soil occurs... could such an invasion come not only from the air, ground and sea, but from below as well? Take note that Oklahoma City is supposed to be one of the 'biggie' NWO transfer points when things get rolling, or so the 'Commu-Nazi's' running the New World Order plot hope. There are some who believe that the U.N. - N.W.O. forces are attempting to precipitate internal civil crisis' in America as a pretext to bringing in multi-national U.N. "peace-keeping" forces to restore "order", that is, the "New World" type of "Order". If there is too much resistance, then a possible U.N.-backed invasion by U.N. member countries -- many of whom despise America anyway thanks to the likes of the CIA -- will be initiated to help these "peace-keepers".

When I couple this information to my own research regarding underground tunnels and secret basis, it becomes clear that there is an unground civilization of which we have little if any information. It would appear that Dulce Base is just one of a large number of hidden bases.

CHAPTER TEN
AN INTERESTING INTERVIEW

Following is yet another article regarding Phil Schneider. Although not written by Schneider himself, the following is an interview with a woman who was aquatinted with the late underground base technician. Although many of the joint CIA-Alien bases have no 'obvious' or overt surface presence or facilities -- for instance Deep Springs, CA; Mercury, NV; Page, AZ; Dulce, NM -- OTHER underground facilities involved with the joint Bavarian-Alien New World Order agenda, aside from those existing below most of the active and 'deactivated' military bases, DO include surface facilities, and some of these for some strange reason are located directly below major Air Port terminals. For instance there is a large underground FEMA base below the Salt Lake City airport; another apparently exists at the Oklahoma City airport which serves as a joint FEMA - UNITED NATIONS "New World Order" detention/transfer center; however the most unusual 'Airport' of this nature seems to be the newer Denver International Airport, as described in the following interview]:

Leading Edge Research: The KSEO 4/26/96 Interview with Alex Christopher. Extract from Leading Edge International Research Journal #92. The KSEO 4/26/96 Interview with Alex Christopher, Author of "Pandora's Box" and "Pandora's Box II". Transcript 6/1/96 by Leading Edge Research Group. Legend: DA [Dave Alan, Host] AC: [Alex Christopher] C: [Caller]

DA: My special guest tonight is Alex Christopher, author of "Pandora's Box", an expose of the British instigation through Washington D.C. over the last 200 years (or more precisely, British-based Masonry, and most notably Scottish Rite Masonry which has long-since infiltrated British and American Masonry. - Branton). You thought you were free? This stuff has been going on forever. The idea was to make us perceive we were "free and independent"... She has a lot of information here, and we are going to have to have her back again for more. I talked to her last night. Just a fascinating individual. She is going to talk about the Montauk Project and extraterrestrial influences, and more. So, Alex, where do you start?

AC: Somebody told me one time, start in the middle and go from there. If you want to, pick a subject and we'll start from there.

DA: Last night we talked about a few things. We talked about the Denver airport last night and what is really going on down there, and we talked a bit about the Montauk project and Al Bielek, and then we skipped around a bit about some of the things in Pandora's Box. You mentioned that the Queen of England has been buying up a lot of property in Colorado under a pseudonym. Why don't we start on the subject of the British? (Note: according to former British Intelligence agent Dr. John Coleman, the London-based Wicca Mason lodges are one-third of the overall global conspiracy. The other two thirds are the Black Nobility banking families who claim direct descent from the early Roman emperors, and also the Maltese Jesuits or the Jesuit - Knights of Malta network. All three networks each have 13 representatives within the Bilderberg organization, which is a cover for the Bavarian Illuminati, suggestive that Bavaria itself has orchestrated a "marriage of convenience" between these three formerly competitive global control groups. - Branton)

AC: All right. The information, primarily, that is in "Pandora's Box" covers how the major corporations, railroad and banking concerns in this country were set up through a 'trust' that was originally known as the Virginia Company... The deal was that everything would remain under English control, or subservient to it, and that brings us right up to today, because we are still looking at everything falling under that 'trust' system going back to the Crown of England. It is mind boggling to think that everyone in this country has been led to believe that the people in the United States had won independence from England, when in fact they never did.

DA: Well, look at President Bush, wherein two years ago he went to England and was knighted by the Queen. Where is that coming from? Is it that he was a faithful servant? (Bush is allegedly a high-level Mason, and a member of the neo-Masonic Skull & Bones lodge. - Branton)

AC: You bet. All of them are doing the bidding, and it goes back to their secret societies and the establishment of the

New World Order, which all leads back to the house of Windsor. There has been in this country for a long time a grooming process whereby people carry on the bidding of the Crown of England. (I did incidentally have somewhat of a confirmation of this when a friend told me that an American judge confided to her that the judicial system in America is now based after the monarchical judicial court systems of England. - Branton) That is one of the things the system involving the Rhodes Scholars was set up to achieve. Cecil Rhodes set it up to groom people for this task, to carry the United States into the New World Order. It appears, from what I have been able to find out, that the Crown of England has had this very skillfully planned for hundreds of years, and it could be possible that they have been privy to information that not many of us have been [privy to] for a long, long time, about the chaos involving Earth changes that are coming. It is my understanding that England is not going to make it through the changes, so they set up a whole new Empire over here. That goes back to some of the things we discussed before, about lands being bought up in Colorado.

(Note: With the fascination Britons have with time-travel, "DR. WHO" and so-on, is it possible that British intelligence could have gained a glimpse into the future and 'seen' what was coming? The Britons have British Columbia, Canada as their possession -- if they are so desperate and convinced that their nation will not survive the 'changes', then why not move the British Empire to B.C. rather than risk offending Americans by opening old wounds that date back to the revolutionary war, and losing their World War I and World War II allies in the process? Just as in America, it is not the general CITIZENS of Britain who pose a threat to freedom, it is the so-called 'elite', the Rockefellers of America and the Rothschilds of Britain who would and have SOLD-OUT their own peoples for personal gain and god-like domination over the lower classes. The Americans and Britons who fought and died together on the battlefields of World War I and II did not realize that the Rothschild-Rockefeller monarchies were the ones who had betrayed them by helping to CREATE the 'monster' that they were fighting in both world wars for the sole purpose of gaining even greater wealth and power. In the end it all came down to base human greed! America has strayed a long ways from the ideals established by the founders of the U.S. Constitution. And, needless to say, Britain has strayed a long ways from the ideals established by the legendary King Arthur whose greatness came from his ability to make all of his knights equals amidst the 'round-table' rather than succumb to vainglory and the temptation of establishing himself as some kind of human deity. Whether the legend of King Arthur was based on fact or not, the IDEALS themselves are nether-the-less real and true. - Branton).

DA: Yes, the area is of a pretty high altitude, where it will be safe.

AC: Yes. Plus, all the symbolism that is apparent in the layout of the new Denver airport says that it is "a control center for world control". There is a lot of "secret society" symbology at the airport. We started researching all of this to find out what it all means. It's all very scary. A gentleman by the name of Al Bielek, who has been involved in some very unusual government projects in the past, told me that "the Denver area is where the establishment of the Western sector of the New World Order will be in the United States". Little bits and pieces keep coming to me, confirming things I have not had confirmed before.

DA: Do you know of John Coleman?

AC: The Committee of 300?

DA: Yes. What's your take on that?

AC: I think his information is fantastic. If he had had the information that I put in "Pandora's Box" when I put that together, it would have blown his mind. But, as far as I know from my standpoint, both sets of material go hand in hand, right down the line.

DA: Some of these things about the background of the British invasion, taking over the land over here while they let us think that we are running this country. How they had a bone to pick with the Czar of Russia years ago, how they have pushed the socialist revolution....like they say, the sun never sets on British soil. About some of these things on the airport in Denver. Would you mind discussing some of those things again?

AC: Well, the first thing that got my attention at the airport was the 'capstone' that I saw in a photograph that had a Masonic symbol on it. So, I really wanted to go to the airport and see that, because I thought it was very unusual.

DA: The capstone?

AC: The capstone, or the dedication stone, for the Denver airport has a Masonic symbol on it. A whole group of us went out to the airport to see some friends off and see this capstone, which also has a time capsule imbedded inside it. It sits at the south eastern side of the terminal which, by the way, is called "The Great Hall", which is what Masons refer to as their meeting hall. And, on this thing it mentions "the New World Airport Commission". I have never heard of that, have you?

DA: Never.

AC: It has a Masonic symbol on it, and it also has very unusual geometric designs. It depicts an arm rising up out of it that curves at a 45 degree angle. It also has a thing that looks like a keypad on it. This capstone structure is made of carved granite and stainless steel, and it is very fancy. This little keypad area at the end of the arm has an out-of-place unfinished wooden block sitting on it. The gentleman that was with me on the first trip out to the airport has since died. They say he committed suicide, but everything else tells me that this is not possible. No one can double-tie a catheter behind his own neck and strangle himself. I just don't think that is possible. But, his name was Phil Schneider, and he started blowing the whistle on all this stuff going on in the underground bases that he had helped build for years and years. He worked on the underground bases at Area 51 and Dulce, New Mexico, as well as several other places. Schneider told me that this keypad-looking area looked like a form of techno-geometry that is "alien-oriented", and that it had something to do with a "directional system", whatever that meant, that functioned as a homing beacon to bring ships right into the "Great Hall".

In the same general area on this capstone, there are some most unusual designs on the floor that are all Masonic in nature, which lead right back to the "Black Sun" [Editor Note: According to Al Bielek, Schneider's father was a U-boat captain during the Nazi regime who was also on the Eldridge in 1943 in a medical capacity], which goes back to Nazi symbology. See, the "secret societies" are supposedly into Sun worship. The Nazi's were into "Black Sun" worship, which connects with the idea of Saturn. Saturn and Satanism kind of go hand-in-hand. (Note: The "Black

Sun" also refers to the massive black hole at the center of our galaxy. In regards to "unusual designs on the floor", one source claims that the base of the Hoover Dam near Las Vegas, not far from Area 51, contains "wild inlays" of occultic and masonic zodiacal symbolism. Reports stated that as the cliffs were being blasted open to make way for the dam, huge caverns were penetrated. Could these have connections with the underground network? Another unusual dam is the Glen Canyon dam near Page, Arizona which could conceivably provide hydroelectric power to a base that allegedly lies below the area and ties the Dulce and Area 51 bases together subterraneally. - Branton) Then, we have this system of murals at the airport that are the most grotesque things you've ever seen.

DA: What's on the murals?

AC: I say that they are about what they plan to do to us, and the world as a whole, not what has happened or some fantasy. One of them that is very unusual has three caskets with dead people in them...

DA: That's part of the ritual connected with the Skull & Bones Club.

Yes. There are evidently three groups of people that they would like to see dead. The first casket has what the artist told me was a Jewish-American child, a little girl, and she has the 'star' on her clothes and a little Bible and a locket... (this may be a depiction of both Judeo-Christian believers, both of whom have historically been the target of the 'inquisitions' of some of the more occultic secret societies of Europe, such as the Thule-backed inquisition against the Jews and the Jesuit-backed inquisition against the Protestants. - Branton)

DA: Jewish lineage is passed through the female...

AC: Yes. Well, all these caskets depict women who are dead. Then, in the center casket there is depicted a Native American woman, and the last casket has a black woman in it. Now, normally I would not have thought too much about these murals if I had not done a lot of research. Even in the government documents I have run across gene-splicing discussions on how they would like to "splice out specific races", and also whoever these people are do not like the Jewish people. This is just one of the murals, and these murals are huge. This same mural depicts the destruction of a city and the forest, and there is a little girl holding a Mayan tablet that speaks of the destruction of civilization. There is a mural that depicts this 'thing' standing over a city that looks like a green "Darth Vader", with a sword, that has destroyed the city. This character is huge, and there is a road depicted with women walking holding dead babies. This same mural extends over to another mural which depicts all of the children of the world taking the weapons from each country on earth and giving them to a central figure which is a GERMAN boy who has this iron fist and anvil in his hand that is totally out of proportion to the child's body, beating the swords into plowshares. I thought, well, this is very odd depicting a German child doing this. What all this symbology on the airport murals seems to convey is that not only do we have a secret society behind this, but that it is a German [Bavarian] secret society behind this, working in the vicinity of this New World Control Center.

DA: It is interesting when you consider Operation Paperclip wherein all these Nazi's were brought to the United States to be groomed, financed, and basically brought back into power.

(Note: That is, by the Rockefeller cartel who supplied Nazi Germany with the oil and materials necessary to keep their war machine operating. Rockefeller-connected OIL companies include EXXON, ARCO, ZAPATA, etc. It is alleged that these corporations initially took in and gave refuge to some 3000 Nazi SS war criminals by providing them with immunity, new identities, and positions within the Bavarian-backed Rockefeller corporate empire and within the CIA -- with the help of Bavarian agents like Allen Dulles, Otto Skorzeny, Reinhardt Gehlen and later Vice President Nelson Rockefeller. These were then used as a covert force to destroy American independence and make America subject to a Bavarian-backed New World Order. Remember even through the Bilderbergers consist of a "marriage of convenience" between Londonese Wicca Masons, Basilian Black Nobility and Roman Maltese Jesuits... the supreme controllers of the Bildeberger cult itself are the secret black gnostic cults of Bavaria whose 'Cult of the Serpent' -- or Illuminati -- can be traced back to Egypt and ultimately to Babylon itself. These Rockefeller-Nazi projects reportedly continued through at least 1975 during which period many thousands more "underground Nazis" were brought into America from Europe and also, if we are to believe some reports, from the secret German

"New Berlin" base under the mountains of Neu Schwabenland, Antarctica that was established during World War II via Nazi-occupied South Africa. Is Neu Schwabenland the REAL power behind the joint Bavarian-Alien New World Order Agenda? The fact that British and American Masons would be pulled into a Bavarian-backed New World Order conspiracy run by anti-British Nazi's and anti-Masonic Jesuits -- in spite of the animosities of World Wars I and II -- would seem contradictory to the extreme. However NOT if we consider the fact that Roman Jesuits had secretly created the Scottish Rite of Masonry at the Jesuit college of Clermont in France and also the Bavarian Illuminati via the Jesuit Adam Weishaupt. Both the Illuminati and Scottish Rite worked together to INFILTRATE Masonry and subdue the traditional Judeo-Christian York Rite. The Masonic elitists in Great Britain and America would have as a result of this infiltration become subject to the influences of the Scottish Rite dominated 33rd degree -- falsely believing that 'Masonry' was still the enemy of the 'Jesuits', as in earlier times the conflict between the two was notorious. They might have been deceived into believing that 'British Masonry' would come out on top of the New World Order when in fact Rome and Bavaria, the two power-centers of the old

[Un]Holy Roman Empire, had the REAL control. But blinded by their own delusions of grandeur and world domination, the British elite failed to see how their Masonic lodges were being infiltrated and manipulated by their sworn enemies. Some of the elite might have been oblivious to the ins-and-outs of Masonry altogether, being conscious only of their own greed. - Branton)

AC: Well, I know they're here, because I have seen them [Germans] alongside the Americans in the more sensitive areas of the airport. But, these paintings are most disturbing and very unusual. When I first tried to contact the artist and talk to him about these murals, he told me that he was given guidelines on what to paint and put in the murals. When I showed up in his studio, I asked to see the guidelines for the last two murals he was working on, he suddenly went "brain dead" and said "of course, there are no guidelines." It took myself and two other people over eight months to figure out all the symbology that is embodied in these murals. It turned out that some of these are 'trigger' pictures, containing symbology designed to trigger altered personalities of people that have been groomed in MKULTRA type programs for specific tasks that they have been trained to do in terms of something connected with Satanic rituals and mind control. I had one woman that called me out of the blue one night, and she was really disturbed about some information. She told me many different things that later turned out to be known MKULTRA triggers. Also, almost every aspect of these murals contains symbols relating back to secret societies. When you get the overall view of what they are talking about in these things, it is very, very scary. It goes back to the Bio-diversity Treaty, getting rid of specific races of people, taking over the world and mind control.

There is one picture in which every plant turns out to be mind-altering or poisonous, and all the animals are Masonic symbols used in literature in every country in the world. It took a very long time to track all this stuff down and figure out what they're trying to say. The one way they tell stories is in pictures. It's right there in our face when you go into the airport. Most people look at them and say, "those are crazy-looking pictures, what are they doing in this airport?"

DA: Now, you mentioned that underneath this airport it goes down many levels.

AC: Yes.

DA: Does the fact that all these underground levels are there have something to do with why it took so long for this airport to open?

AC: Well, the gentleman that I was dealing with, Phil Schneider said that during the last year of construction they were connecting the underground airport system to the deep underground base. He told me that there was at least an eight-level deep underground base there, and that there was a 4.5 square mile underground city and an 88.5 square-mile base underneath the airport. It is very unusual that they would allot a 50 square-mile area on the surface at which to locate an airport in the middle of nowhere unless they really planned to use it for something very unusual later. There is a 10-mile, 4-line highway out to this airport, and there is nothing out there in between the airport and Denver. Not even a service station, at least in September 1995. The people in Denver are really upset with the fact that this airport went in the way it did.

There was this fellow who wrote a book in which he made the statement that they had a copy of an audio tape on which a Denver city official was talking with people from the CIA, and that he was paid 1.5 million dollars to allow the 'airport' to be built, no matter what it took. It appears that there was a lot more interest in getting the airport built from just officials in the Denver area. They plan on using this facility for something else other than just landing planes.

DA: So, this guy got you down there to take a look at the underground?

AC: Well, he was invited to go along on the trip. I had a friend that actually got us down into the active area in the underground. It's very interesting down there. The baggage equipment area is very unusual. All the old luggage equipment that wouldn't work right doesn't look much different than the stuff that is working today.

DA: You were telling me that there are huge concrete corridors with sprinklers all along the ceiling. What are these sprinkler heads doing in a concrete bunker, pray tell? (Presumably concrete will not 'burn' if there is a potential fire, so is it possible that something other than 'water' is meant to be expelled from these sprinklers which are located "all along" the ceiling? - Branton)

AC: Well, this is the same question we asked. These shafts are huge and run along adjacent to the tramline on both sides. So, there are two of these huge shafts large enough to fit a two-lane highway in there. There are very FEW openings into and out of the tram shaft, but at the end of them, going out into this 50 square miles of acreage is a huge steel door that would facilitate the entrance of a great big truck. It could be used for almost anything, but what is so unusual about it is that about EVERY FIVE OR SIX FEET on the ceiling, across almost the full width of the area, there is a pipe with three or four sprinkler heads. This goes on for the FULL length of the thing, "which must be close to a mile". There are two of these shafts, and I got a picture in the mail the other day which was very unusual that was taken by someone on board the tram in the shaft. The picture appeared to actually show ghost-like figures on it. It was a mother and a baby wrapped in a blanket. When you are down in that concrete shaft, both times I got nauseated. There are some very unusual vibrations down there (from other 'time dimensions'? - Branton). Now, the tunnel shaft that the tram comes in on could connect up with an underground tunnel coming in from five buildings that were built and buried. There was already a 40 foot diameter tunnel there when construction started. Those five buildings they built 3 1/2 years ago, and suddenly they said "oops, these are in the wrong place", and buried them, along with a very high-tech runway that is buried under about four inches of dirt. It seems insane that they would build a very technical building complex with interlocking tunnels and a tunnel going back to the tram tunnel at the concourse, and then state that they built it in the "wrong place" and cover it up with dirt. I don't believe that people are that stupid.

DA: No. Projects like that are strategically planned, and they just don't go and do that.

AC: Some of these five buildings are 150 feet tall. There is one 78 feet tall, and one that is 126 feet tall. They are all in that range. From this complex there is a shaft that runs to concourse "C". When they started this project, as I said, there was also a huge 40 foot diameter shaft brought in there from somewhere that was off-limits to the work crews. It was there when the project was started. And, everybody that worked on these projects....there were five different contractors, and the people on each contracted crew did not interact with the other ones. When the project was done, everyone was fired and sent away.

DA: You would think that during this massive construction they would not be able to keep this stuff secret.

AC: I think a lot of the people saw things that disturbed them so much that they would not talk about it. I know several people who worked on the project that managed to find their way down into the depths, probably close to the deep underground base, and saw things that scared them so badly they won't talk about it. I interviewed a few of the former employees on these construction crews that worked out there on these buildings that ended up buried, and they are afraid to talk. They say that everybody is real nervous about it, and they decided to tell some of the secrets that they knew, but they don't want anybody to know who they are. So, I can tell you that it is a very unusual and spooky type of place, and if you are a sensitive person you get nauseated as soon as you enter the perimeter of the airport. Especially when you go down underground. You become very nauseated a nervous. There is also so much electromagnetic flux in the area that if you get out on the open ground around the airport, you will 'buzz'.

DA: Where is this flux field coming from? What do you think the purpose of this is?

AC: I think that it's coming from some kind of underground electrical system, because where we were there were no power lines, and the whole place was just buzzing with this free energy floating around. Very unusual. In addition, there are areas in the underground that have chain-link fences with the barbed wire tops pointed inward, like they were there to keep people in, not keep people out. All these areas are there, acres of it, and none of it is in active use. There are many terraced areas that go down. One area in particular is forbidden to go into unless you are wearing a biological protective suit. They say there is some kind of "unidentified biological fungus" in that area that attacks people's lungs.

DA: Hmmm. Some kind of way to hide something that is in this area?

AC: Well, we think that area is one that leads to deeper levels underground at the airport. But, it is surrounded by a chain-link fence and you can't get in there. We think this is the area that one of the electricians kind of stumbled into that went down about six levels below the fourth level, and ran into some really weird stuff. He won't talk about any of it now.

DA: Real weird stuff.

AC: Also, at the airport there are what look like miniature nuclear reactor cooling towers, and I don't understand why they are there. When people asked, the reply is that they are part of the ventilation and exhaust system. Ventilation and exhaust from where?

DA: What do you think it's for?

AC: I think it is all hooked up to the deep underground.

DA: They say that this place looks like some underground "holding area"...somewhat like a cattle lot....a place that could hold thousands of people. The gates, fences....

AC: The luggage transport vehicles move on a full-sized double-lane highway, and along this highway are chain-linked areas that could be used for holding areas. I don't understand why they built this the way they did, unless they planned to use it for something like that in the future.

DA: So what could all this be for?

AC: If Phil is right, and all this hooks up to the deep underground base that he was offered the plans to build back in 1979, and that what this other man TOLD me in private [is] that there is a lot of human SLAVE LABOR in these deep underground bases being used by these aliens, and that a lot of this slave labor is children. HE SAID that when the children reach the point that they are unable to work anymore, they are slaughtered on the spot and consumed.

DA: Consumed by who?

AC: Aliens. Again, this is not from me, but from a man that gave his life to get this information out. He worked down there for close to 20 years, and he knew everything that was going on.

DA: Hmmm. Who do these aliens eat?

AC: They specifically like young human children, that haven't been contaminated like adults. Well, there is a gentleman out giving a lot of information from a source he gets it from, and he says that there are an incredible number of children snatched in this country.

DA: Over 200,000 each year.

AC: And that these children are the main entree for dinner.

(Note: Many will read this and scoff in utter disbelief at such a claim. This is all well and fine, and even Phil Schneider warns us to put on our 'skepticals' when investigating claims and to investigate them so that they can be definitively proven one way or the other, as all claims of an extraordinary nature should be. So, I would suggest that Congress by-pass the EXECUTIVE branch of government -- which has sold-out to the Intelligence-Military-Industrial Complex, a branch that was originally intended by the founders of the Republic to be the 'servants' of CONGRESS, the SENATE and the PEOPLE -- and undertake a full-scale investigation of this and other underground bases, even if this calls for full-scale Congress-backed military mobilization. The excuse for such an undertaking could for instance be to investigate claims of unethical use of U.S. tax dollars, violations of Federal Medical Regulations in regards to genetic research, failure to pay property taxes on underground facilities used by non-elected officials, harboring of "illegal aliens", bribery and treason, illegal cattle rustling in regards to the Dulce and other bases, possible kidnapping and human rights abuses against children, and so on... - Branton)

DA: How many Draconians are down there?

AC: I have heard the figure of 150,000 just in the New York area.

DA: Underneath New York?

AC: Yes. In some kind of underground base there.

DA: Interesting. Now, you've seen pictures of these things?

AC: I have seen them face to face.

DA: You have?

AC: Yes. From some information that has been put out by a group or team that also works in these underground bases that is trying to get information out to people that love this country, THERE IS A WAR THAT IS GOING ON UNDER OUT FEET, AND ABOVE OUR HEADS, that the public doesn't know anything about, and it's between these ALIEN forces and the HUMANS that are trying to fight them.

DA: What other types have you seen?

AC: The ones that I have seen are the big-eyed Greys and the Reptilians.

DA: What do these Reptilians look like?

AC: There are three different types.

DA: Can you tell us how you happened to come into contact with them?

AC: When I lived in Florida in Panama City, at that particular time the Gulf Breeze sightings were going on, and the area was virtually a hotbed for strange events. I had neighbors that were into watching UFOs and getting information about them. One night about 2:30 am, my neighbor called me and was absolutely frantic, and wanted me to come over there. I ran over there and went in the front door, and she and her boyfriend, who is a commercial airline pilot, were in the living room scared out of their wits. I looked over at her, and her eyeballs are rolling back in her head and she was passing out and sliding down the wall. Her boyfriend was trying to tell me what was going on, and I was feeling this incredible energy that felt like it was trying to penetrate my head. So, I grabbed both of them and pulled them both outside, where we stood for a while and talked...

DA: Some people would say that this is a case of demon possession...

AC: Oh, no. There was radiation in the room. The next day all of her plants were dead. So, there was a massive amount of energy focused on that room. Anyway, after about an hour had passed, we had discussed what went on and decided to go back into the house. They had both been in bed and were pulled out of their bed during the night. All they remember is a flash of light in their faces and the next thing they know they're both scared to death. But, when we went back into the house, I noticed that the man had a small palm-print on his side with fingers that must have been 10 inches long, with claw marks on the end that were burned into his side. The next day, that area was so swollen that he could not touch it. I have video pictures of these things on his side. The prints were there from someone bending down from behind him and pulling him out of bed. They had been making love, and 'somebody' lifted him off of her and left these burns there.

Anyway, they were both totally flipped out. I finally got them calmed down enough to let me go home. I went home and went to bed. The next thing I know, I woke up and there is this 'thing' standing over my bed. He had wrap-around yellow eyes with snake pupils, and pointed ears and a grin that wrapped around his head. He had a silvery suit on, and this scared the living daylights out of me. I threw the covers over my head and started screaming....I mean, here is this thing with a Cheshire-cat grin and these funky glowing eyes...this is too much. I have seen that kind of being on more than one occasion.

DA: What else can you say about it?

AC: Well, he had a hooked nose and he was [humanoid] looking, other than the eyes, and had kind of grayish skin. Later on in 1991, I was working in a building in a large city, and I had taken a break about 6:00, and the next thing I knew it was 10:30 at night, and I thought I had taken a short break. I started remembering that I was taken aboard a ship, through four floors of an office building, and through a roof. There on the ship is where I encountered 'GERMANS' AND 'AMERICANS' WORKING TOGETHER, and also the GREY ALIENS, and then we were taken to some other kind of facility and there I saw the REPTILIANS again ... the one's I call the "baby Godzilla's", that have the short teeth and yellow slanted eyes, and who look like a Velociraptor, kind of.

DA: So, why would these people pick on you?

AC: Well, I found one common denominator in the abduction, and it keeps on being repeated over and over again. I deal with lots of people who have been abducted, and the one common denominator seems to be the blood line, and it's the blood line that goes back to ancient Indian or Native American blood lines.

DA: Are these people looking for genetic material?

AC: Well, I don't know if it is a very ancient blood line that they want to try and stop, or what the reasoning is. I know that I was asked some questions, like how I was capable of doing some of the psychic things I was doing at the time. But, it is very unusual to find anybody that remotely thinks they have been taken that doesn't have the Indian blood line, somewhere.

DA: Now, after that experience, what happened after that? What were some of the other times you saw some of these beings?

AC: Well, at that facility I saw the almond-eyed Greys, but the thing that sticks in my mind are the beings that look like reptiles, or the velociraptors. They are the cruelest beings you could ever imagine, and they even smell hideous. There were a couple of very unusual areas down there where I was taken which looked like cold storage lockers, where these things were in hibernation tubes, and that is about all I remember, other than seeing some black helicopters and little round-wing disk type aircraft. At that point, the memory seems to be cut off and I can't tap through to anything else. They're there, folks.

DA: Maybe I'll open up some phone lines, and maybe we'll talk about Al Bielek and some things you discussed with him. Are you open to that?

AC: Sure.

Caller (C): On those ships where the Germans and Americans were, did they have any kind of an insignia on their uniforms?

AC: Yes, they did. I have been told that the organization is called "The Black League" (possibly the "Black Monks" within the NSA who reportedly interact directly with aliens? - Branton); by people that might know. A blue triangle with a red-eyed black dragon, with a circle around it. It was very unusual. There's another woman that has written a book about an encounter she had in Fort Walden.

I met her some years back, and we were taking about things we've seen. She also talked about this strange insignia. She and I both sat down and drew what we saw, and they were virtually carbon copies of each other. (Note: Winged serpent symbols have been observed by several abductees, including policeman Herbert Schirmer who reported the insignia on the uniforms of the reptilian-eyed grays that had abducted him. - Branton)

In the book "Cosmic Conflict", the author talks about the ancient city that was uncovered by the Germans before World War II, and tells about their effort to revive some frozen humans they found in this underground city, and that the true humans couldn't be revived, but the ones that could be revived were in fact reptilians in disguise, and the reptilians have the capability to do shape-shifting and create a [laser] holographic image so when you look at them you see a human, but under that there is no human there. It's like a "deja vu" of the movie "They Live". (Note: An early newsletter called THE CRYSTAL BALL published information along this line, which stated that the Soviets had during the investigation of a meteor crash uncovered a buried city in Siberia where they discovered the frozen bodies of both humans -- who could NOT be revived, and human-appearing reptilians -- who WERE revived from the frozen state. Allegedly the reptilians re-animated and killed the Soviet scientists and through some type of psychic osmosis drained their minds and assimilated their memories and features through a molecular shape-shifting type process. John Carpenter, who directed THEY LIVE, also directed an earlier movie called THE THING which was based somewhat on a similar theme. The alien 'impostors' then called for backup and more scientists came out and were 'replaced', and these eventually returned to Russia and began to infiltrate the Communist government. Although such claims may seem preposterous, it is nevertheless interesting how numerous 'preposterous' claims as this contain identical 'reptilian' themes. Aside from the instinctive and basic racial fear in humans of things 'reptilian', could this re-occurring theme be more than mere coincidence? - Branton) Cathy O'Brien, who wrote "Trance-Formation in America", revealed that George Bush projected a hologram that he was a reptilian .... real crazy stuff, but if this technology that they possess is there, why couldn't a race do something like that ... these 'people' that are working with our government?

C: I believe that, but I do believe that these are demons that manifest themselves as alien beings, and that this has been going on for a long time...

DA: Demons? Who are demons?

C: Fallen angels.

DA: The reptilians look like that anyway. All the scriptures around the planet talk about serpent beings (or in the case of Judeo-Christian scriptures like Genesis chapter 3 and Revelation chapter 12, serpent beings possessed by 'demons' or through which demons are able to or allowed to 'incarnate'. - Branton) What do you think, Alex?

AC: Well, I think that's pretty much what the bottom line is. Also, they talk about the rapture...

DA: It could be like an alien 'thanksgiving'.

AC: These people that have done all this research and are part of the underground government are telling that the humans on this planet have been at war with these reptilian aliens for thousands of years. At one point, things got so hot on the planet, like it is now, aliens took on this holographic image and infiltrated the human race in order to take it over and undermine it, just like this New World Order is doing right now. They're saying that the same thing happened to civilization on Earth before, and that the humans before actually had the capability for interplanetary travel, and that it was so bad here with the reptilians that they had to leave... What they are also saying is that these beings that are human-looking that are visiting our planet, at this time, trying to inform people what is going on, and guide them, are actually OUR ANCESTORS THAT ESCAPED FROM EARTH before, when it was under reptilian domination.

DA: What is your take on these crop circles?

AC: Oh, the crop circles that are the real ones are a type of geometric language containing some kind of information. There was one that was a Mandelbrot fractal. How do you fake that? They say that there are a lot of crop circles going on in the United States, and that the government shuts the information off (or destroys the crop circles before the public can find them, others claim. - Branton) about their occurrence.

DA: Canada and Australia as well.

C: It seems that we are having an increase in these encounters and sightings.

AC: Things are escalating at an incredible rate. I think a lot of these movies in the media are trying to get us softened up for what they plan to unleash on us.

C: So, in just a matter of years, they plan to bring it out and bring people to that airport?

AC: You know, Reagan said more than once that the only thing that would bring people together would be some kind of "outside force".

DA: Exactly, I remember that. He said that several times.

AC: I went to South Florida a couple of weeks ago and interviewed a man who had done research for 30 years, and oddly enough, he tapped into some of the same information I had, in that our government has had round-winged, saucer-type technology, high mach speed aircraft since the

1920's, and that in 1952 they had over 500 of these aircraft hidden in secret bases. Now, if they had that in 1952, considering that military technology grows by 44 years for every year that goes by, what do you imagine they have now, 44 years later, after technology has advanced the equivalent of 1,936 years?

C: About two or three months ago, I went to do a business transaction with a fellow I have known for about two or three years, and one of his relatives had just died -- we were pretty close, and we got into a deep conversation about stuff, and he told me he worked in an underground military base in Colorado. I asked him what he did there, and he said that if he told me he'd have to kill me. I told him I didn't want to know. I was really shocked, and didn't know what to think of it, and then I heard this program. I want to know what your guest thinks about the Iron Mountain report the government did in the 1960's, and if that ties into the Nazis and the Americans [CIA] working together. Also, this would also explain George Washington's vision where this country was invaded from the East by a foreign power, and then when all hope seemed lost, the angels of God would come down and the nation would be saved. Anyway, I never could understand why angels of God would come down and fight with men to save a puny little country that has been around for only 200 years, but in this scenario, there seems to be some explanation here.

AC: Yes, the Iron Mountain report. The guy that claims to be the author of it now claims that it was nothing more than a joke, but for a joke, it seems to be following the time line to the hilt, so I think it was something that made its way out and they are trying to cover that up. Everything that was in that report is happening in great detail right now.

C: Do these reptilians bleed if they get shot?

DA: Has anybody ever killed one?

AC: Phil Schneider did. He killed several of them. When he was involved in cutting some tunnels at Dulce, he was lowered down a shaft and ended up in a nest of these things. He and some of his team were in there, and some of the Delta Force came in. They had a shootout with these aliens, and he killed a couple of them before they got a round off and shot him with some sort of laser weapon. He used to pull his shirt up and show me where they darned near blew a hole in his chest with whatever kind of laser weapon they were using.

DA: So they can be killed, then?

AC: Yes, if you have the drop on them. They die just like everyone else. They consist of mass just like we do.

C: It is interesting that high officials in the Clinton administration, like Cisneros, were deeply involved with the construction of this airport. Also, Pat Schroeder. All of a sudden, she's leaving office. It's like a lot of people who have been involved with this airport are leaving town. Also, there is a fellow by the name of Rodney Stitch, who writes about the total corruption in the Denver area. Does this tie in with what you were talking about?

AC: Well, he is the one that wrote the book "Defrauding America". He said that they had a tape of a CIA agent paying off the mayor of Denver to get the airport built. There is just so much corruption. They are selling the good American people out. We have some of our own people selling the rest of population out for a few pieces of gold.

DA: What about Al Bielek and how what he is saying may relate to this?

AC: I met Al about a year ago.

DA: Who is Al Bielek?

AC: He claims to be one of the ones who jumped overboard off the Eldridge when it went into hyperspace during the Philadelphia Experiment. He actually traveled forward in time, and asked the people that he encountered there what happened in his future. At that time, he was given the information about the New World Order and that Denver was the location for the NWO Western Sector, and that Atlanta was supposed to be the control center for the Eastern Sector. Can it be that the fact that the Olympics is supposed to be in Atlanta is part of a scenario? All the highways in Atlanta have high-security monitoring cameras just like those seen in some of the underground areas at the Denver airport. These monitors are all over the interstate highway and on many of the streets in Atlanta. Last week, I was talking to a fellow who was actually working on the Olympic project, in terms of the main stadium, and he said that they're gearing up for the possibility of terrorist acts. Do they know something we don't know?

(Note: As for 'Denver' being the center of a New World Order control system in the west, we should realize that the future is not fully SET. It IS subject to change. There are, according to contactees, different 'parallel realities' that exist. The 3rd dimensional or 3rd density reality is the 'foundation' upon which all others exist. Other realities exist in 4th, 5th and other 'densities' wherein objects and events are somewhat more 'fluid' than in 3rd dimensional reality. Many who claim to have traveled in time state that while doing so they were out-of-phase somewhat with the people within the other time-zones. They could observe them yet were 'invisible' or in a phased-out state, in essence unable to 'interfere' to the point of changing 3rd dimensional past events. Others, involved in the Montauk project for instance, state that the 'futures' that they observed were of a quasi-reality or semi-dreamlike nature, as if 'future' reality was like wet clay that had not yet 'set' and solidified into a CONCRETE reality. So if this is the case, then Denver does NOT necessarily have to be a New World Order control center, even though the 'thought forms', or what you might call 'reality blueprints', ARE being created by the secret government and are in the process of 'solidifying' as the future gets closer. However, ANY thought form can be destroyed and replaced BEFORE it solidifies into 3rd density concrete reality. Those living within the 3rd density event-flow have the POWER to determine the outcome of events through their connection to the eternal NOW, just as a large river has first priority over the smaller tributaries in determining the course of a river bed. So then we are living in an eternal NOW which is continually in the process of being converted from a FLUID thought form state and into CONCRETE material form state. Once 'set', an event cannot be undone. However if there is even a minimal amount of malleability left to the event, then that event can potentially be turned... for better or worse. - Branton)

DA: Maybe they want to go ahead and perpetrate something again. One thing after another. It's all part of their scenario. Let's take a call.

C: Yes, I would like to thank you and your guest for coming forward with this information. And, as unbelievable as it is for the audience, I personally have had first-hand experience with some of this stuff. Not so much with the reptilians, but when you talk about this technology base that the government is working with, my own encounters with this technology were basically terrifying, in that I didn't know what was going on. I got indoctrinated into some type of mind control program that was perpetrated on me. I was in the wrong place at the wrong time. It's amazing to me that this stuff is going on, and I know that it is frustrating to get people to wake up to this. I am a little nervous here. It runs a little deeper than just on a physical level of threat. I think a lot of this stuff is not just about suppressing our minds and will to resist the government. It's about getting our minds to the point to where we're so "droned down" that we have no chance of reconnecting with the source. I think this whole thing has to do with us on a soul level.

AC: That's right. That's what it's all about. It's the last great adventure to control the space between our ears and to eventually take over our souls. I also think that a lot of the people who have sold us out and are involved in this have no idea what the BIG picture is, because it is all so compartmentalized. This is a very demonic scenario that is going on here.

C: That is why I will spend the rest of my days trying to bring this to people's attention. My take on it is that if you don't make the cut when all of this comes to a climax, and they do achieve that ultimate control, your chances of reconnecting are delayed indefinitely.

AC: Well, you know, we have some beings that are waiting for people to ask, in mass, for help, and they are there, and they will help, but we have to ask for help, because they honor free will.

C: My previous experience was pretty nightmarish, but I did get through this, and my perspective on God is a gift.

DA: Alex, how do we get a hold of your book, "Pandora's Box"?

AC: You can write to PANDORA'S BOX, 2663 Valleydale Road, Suite 126, Birmingham, Alabama 35224. "Pandora's Box - Volume One" is $50 [$80 Overseas], and "Pandora's Box - Volume Two" is $35 [$65 Overseas]. The book called "The Cosmic Conflict" is $40 [$75 Overseas]. These are big books, with lots of information.

DA: Well, Alex, thank you for being here, and we'll have you back here again.

CHAPTER ELEVEN

IS IT REAL?

The following document was sent to me with assertions that it is very real. However, with all of the disinformation making the rounds you never know. However, I am submitting it for those who might be interested.

E.D.H.
Earth Defense Headquarters
Technical Brief

Winter - 2001

Edited by

CAPTAIN MARK RICHARDS

Published by - Earth Defense Headquarters

http://www.edhca.org/

Condensed and re-edited by 'BRANTON' with the permission of E.D.H.

This is a greatly condensed version of the 'DULCE BATTLE' Report... The full 166 page version of this --- and other E.D.H. Research Reports --- are available at:

http://www.edhca.org/12.html

Government scientists (the secret government) purportedly labored alongside an alien force to work out the sundry ways the general population could be brought under an ultimate totalitarian control that would leave humanity as little more than farm animals to be used for breeding. All of which began with a 1947 treaty signed by President Harry Truman, that set in motion a plan where the ELITE obtained alien technological secrets in exchange for permitting the aliens to abduct human subjects for their diabolical research. In time, the elite would be allowed to survive to become the overlords of the human sheep, under ultimate control of the aliens - like the dogs that watch the sheep on a human farm...

Located almost two miles beneath Archuleta Mesa on the Jicarilla Apache Indian Reservation near Dulce, New Mexico was an installation classified so secret, its existence would be one of the most protected realities in the world. There was the Earth's first main joint United States Government/Alien biogenetics laboratory. Others existed in Colorado, Nevada, and Arizona, not to mention in a number of other locations like Afghanistan and Russia - but Dulce (is)/was the largest.

In an era when the officers in charge of the major military units were still part of the generation that looked on young women - potential mothers - as a treasure to be protected, to learn that thousands of young females were being abducted, and even created (cloned, etc.) for use as sex slaves by aliens was simply too much for such men to allow to continue.

The turning point came when National Security Adviser Dr. Zbigniew Brzezinski met with President Jimmy Carter in the White House on June 14, 1977, with a number of other "intelligence operatives and leaders", to bring the President up to speed on a number of top secret programs, including "Project Aquarius", and the work being done at Dulce, Area 51, and other secret bases. Brzezinski, a member of the power elite that backed the "Grey" cause, never guessed that the President would be so shocked that he would soon turn to trusted military advisors in the military intelligence community for options of how to stop what had been going on.

The National Security Agency (NSA) had been secretly fighting the alien cause, and the humans that worked for or with the aliens, since it was established in the mid-1950s'. Project Aquarius was originally established in 1953, by order of President Eisenhower, under control of the National Security Council (NSC) and MJ 12. In 1966, the Project's name had been changed from Project Gleem to

Project Aquarius, and portions of it went into DEEP COVER, hidden even from the CIA and the NSC. At that point, the NSA had opened "Department X" (to identify and study all alien or enemy operations that could be a threat to the United States or the Human Race in general), and "Department Z" (to "react" and "neutralize" any sort of threat to the United States or the Human Race).

Under secret Presidential Order, signed by President Jimmy Carter, the NSA's Department Z, the newly established DELTA FORCE, and a hand-picked group of Air Force SOC, Navy SEAL, and Army Rangers were organized for a mission so secret that not even command officers were told what it was about until the night of the attack. The only 'Attack Team' leaders who knew what this would be about were the men involved in the NSA Department Z, who had been involved with fighting aliens for years. The commanding officer of the attack was none other than Captain Mark Richards, the son of the infamous "Dutchman", Major Ellis Loyd Richards, who had been the commander of International Security (IS) since Admiral Chester W. Nimitz died in 1966...

By 1978, the NSA Department X was warning the human commanders of new programs starting at Dulce that were so frightening that even seasoned men of war were shocked. Thousands of young human females were being "created" in test tubes to be sex slaves for the aliens. But these clones were proving to be less than satisfying for the aliens', because they didn't "suffer" the same way that once free victims did. They could be engineered to provide better sexual tools for some of the stranger life forms, but they were proving to be nearly "mindless", and thus couldn't react with the "fear" that normal young women could. For that reason, while the clone program would continue, it had been decided that the abduction program would be stepped up - with the forced "short-term" attacks to increase by 1980 to over 100,000 a year, and the facility to be enlarged for "long-term" victims (who would stay there for as long as they lived) with numbers over 75,000.

The labs at Dulce started cloning human females by a process perfected in the world's largest and most advanced bio-genetic facility, Los Alamos. The elite humans who manipulated the worlds' governments from the shadows would soon have a disposable slave-race, for medical culling of body parts and their own perverted pleasures. Like the alien Greys, the U.S. (secret) Government secretly kidnaped and impregnated young females, then removed the hybrid fetus after a three-month time period, before accelerating their growth in laboratories. Biogenetic (DNA Manipulation) programming was then instilled - many being implanted with all sorts of devices, some that allowed them to be controlled at a distance through RF (Radio Frequency) transmissions...

From: EDH Archives: Dulce Interviews; WC-289487346--80...

"Level 7 is worse... It was like a whore house for pervert ETs'. Human females were brought there for 'experiments', but you can't convince me that most of it wasn't just sadistic pleasure for the Greys. They wouldn't just impregnate the girls; they would sexually torture them for hours. Sure there were the scientific procedures, but there were also orgies where a few pretty human females would be given to a large number of Greys for nothing less than a brutal gang-rape. And this was constant. Hundreds of Greys, and other species that seemed to be friends to the Greys, would come and go every week, for no other clear reason than to take sexual pleasure with the provided human females."

When the truth was evident that sub-humans and other creatures were being produced from abducted human females, impregnated against their will, a secret resistance group formed within the military and intelligence agencies of the U.S. Government that did not approve of the deals that had been made with the 'Off-worlders'. Many of these brave humans would be assassinated, or "died under mysterious circumstance," or would be silenced in other ways. But in 1979, they would manage a victory that would cost the Greys, and the humans that backed the Greys, dearly...

The Air Force Intelligence Officer that reportedly was the man who met with the Aliens at Holloman (Air Force Base) in 1964 was the legendary 'Dutchman,' Ellis Loyd Richards, Jr. - the same man who would reportedly order the attack on Dulce in 1979, and whose son, Captain Mark Richards, would lead the human attack on the facility.

The Richards names come up time and time again when one looks into any of the mentioned Top Secret Projects that Military Intelligence, or the Eyes-Only, Tops Secret agency known as International Security, were involved in from World War II through the Cold War years...

The in-house political argument that developed within MAJESTIC TWELVE in the late 1970s, when the military/intelligence men objected to the deals with some of the Aliens on the side for the selfish gain of such groups as the Illuminati of thousands or the "Club of Rome" at the expense of thousands of innocents, if not all of mankind, helped to cause the rift that would lead to the military action taken against the Dulce facility in 1979...

(Later on in the DULCE BATTLE report, it is written...)

"It would be ONE OF the reptoids who taught several of the men involved in the attack on Dulce a number of the informative points that would first cause them to look more deeply into what was being done at the facility, and then helped them better understand the enemy, and how to defeat them. Indeed, it would be this Reptoid who communicated the factual basis for a number of the plots being organized against humanity by a number of off-world sources, and (some of them) had proven their willingness to aid the human cause in the Battle for Central Asia in 1976, and in the August 1979 space defense of Earth against alien invaders. It was also (they) who warned of the danger that such life forms as bacteria represented to both aliens and humans...

In 1979, there were 37 alien species represented at the Dulce facility. Only 6 of those had their own space or dimensional traveling ability, while the others were guests of the Greys. All of those species that had come as guests of the Greys were there for genetic and reproductive experiments with humans - and 8 of those were also interested in humans as A SOURCE OF FOOD. Of those interested in reproductive experiments, 25 could enjoy direct intercourse with human females (although several needed the female to be placed on special hormone treatments ahead of time), and the facility apparently got the reputation for being a sexual pleasure spot for the quadrant.

Of course, not all the Reptoid-type creatures are friendly towards humans. According to Lear and others, the U.S. government may have made a 'pact' with a non-human race as early as 1933. According to some this 'race' is not human yet claims to have had its origin on Earth... Some sources allege that this predatory race is of a neo-saurian nature. This has led others to suggest that the dinosaurs which ruled the surface of the Earth in prehistoric times may not have become entirely extinct as is commonly believed, but that certain of the more intelligent and biped-hominoid mutations of that race developed a form of intellectual thought equal to, or surpassing (in some respects - especially with their 'collective mind' matrix - Branton) that of the human race...

The theory then suggests that some of this race went into space, only to return to find that their founders on their home planet had not survived (on the surface, that is, however there are several reports of reptilian humanoids being encountered in deep underground natural cavern systems all over the world... and in time, the space-based reptiloids learned of these. - Branton)

There were a number of facts quickly put forward; for instance one branch or mutation of the supposedly extinct sauroid race, Stenonychosaurus, was according to paleontologists remarkably hominoid in appearance, being 3 ½ to 4 ½ feet in height with possibly greyish-green skin and three digit clawed hands and a partially-opposable 'thumb'. The opposable thumb and intellectual capacity are the only thing preventing members of the animal kingdom from challenging the human race as the masters of planet Earth. For instance, the ape kingdom possesses opposable thumbs yet it does not possess the intellectual capacity to use them as humans do. The dolphins possess intellects nearing that of humans but do not possess opposable thumbs or even limbs necessary to build, etc.

The cranial capacity of Stenonychosaurus was nearly twice the size of that of human beings, indicating a large and possibly advanced though not necessarily benevolent intellect.

According to researchers such as Brad Steiger, Val Valerian, TAL Lévesque and others, this may actually be the same type of entity or entities most commonly described in 'UFO' encounters, as well as the same type of creatures depicted in early 1992 in the nationally viewed CBS presentation "INTRUDERS."

According to Lear, the government may have established a 'treaty' with this (reptilian) race, which they later learned to their horror was extremely malevolent in nature and were merely using the 'treaties' as a means to buy time while they methodically established certain controls upon the human race, with the ultimate goal of an absolute domination...

The fact that a base like Dulce might house dozens of 'types' and 'races' of ETs' would never be admitted by most humans, and would be reduced to the stuff of legends if ever turned over to the general public. The years of work to cover up the alien threat had worked very well by 1979, and normal people would not admit seeing an alien for fear of being called crazy.

The types and races at Dulce at the time of the attack are still in question, and many races have not wanted to admit their taking part in what took place there in 1979...

Many victims find their abductors to be nothing less than brutal beasts. The casebooks of researchers are filled with incidents in which malice and hostility played a significant role in the abduction. Unfortunately, most of the victims who suffer these more vile attacks do not get the chance to make any report to any human authority about the event - as they vanish, and become another statistic in the growing number of "missing persons" across the country.

By the early 1970s, the number of these missing persons - most of all, young white women - were going up. While the abductions of humans by superhuman forces of varying descriptions appeared to obey the same mechanisms worldwide, it was clear that young white women were the most frequent victims, and that there was little support for abductees should they survive...

In the more controlled environment of Dulce, researchers had no... disclosure problems (concerning stem cell and cloning research). The fertilized eggs of hundreds of healthy young human females could be 'harvested' constantly, for unlimited embryo and stem-cell research, 'killing' uncounted human embryos in the search for everything from cures to alien skin infections caused by Earth germs, to how to better create a sub-human slave race of cloned worker creatures.

Such research also moved into other dangerous fields, such as 'enhancing' humans into becoming creatures that would serve other alien needs. One of the more shocking of these that the 'attackers' would find in huge holding pens were the human females who had been 'enhanced' to become reproductive 'cows', as the need for human milk and reproductive systems had grown. Hundreds of young women had been 'altered', to become little more than cows...

'Free will' is always dangerous to a fascist society, or a police state! 'Free will' is what allowed a group of men to take the moral high-ground, and attack the Dulce Facility...

The attack plan centering on crippling the main generator, then doing as much damage as possible -- while freeing as many victims as possible -- started to take shape in the Fall of 1979, after the August space battle between forces of the USAF Space Command and an alien invasion force, with none other than Brigadier General Aderholt

(USAF) brought in to head the organization that would be formed for the invasion of the Dulce Facility.

Funded by Texas businessman Ross Perot, CIA/DIA front man Edwin Wilson, and a massive black ops' fund long hidden (by Major E.L. Richards Jr.) the plan moved forward quickly within a small community of intelligence officers and their backers...

Brigadier General Harry C. Aderholt would pull a team together in September and October of 1979 that would have made any commanding officer proud, and perhaps shot fear into any enemy who had any idea of what was being put together. Colonel Roger H.C. Donlon, stationed at Fort Leavenworth at the time, would head one combat team, drawing heavily from the newly formed DELTA FORCE, Navy SEALS, and USAF Special Operations Command (AFSOC). Flight teams were organized by astronaut scientist Karl Gordon Henize, and included the best of the best in combat and test pilots, with special operations training - or who could be counted on to keep their silence, including Captain Mark Richards, who was recovering from his command role of Dragon Squadron in the battle that had taken place in August.

While exact numbers of the human force involved is still so protected that there seems to be no firm record of the exact count, there were never more than a few hundred who knew anything about the operation. The center of the operation was clearly found in USAF Space Command, and the Director of I.S., Major Ellis L. Richards Jr.

The President (of the U.S.), the Secretary General of the United Nations, and the Chairman of the JCS were never informed of the pending operation, and it should be noted that the humans and aliens involved in the attack took part in the action without orders or clearances from higher authorities.

Those who fought against the aliens did so against the will of the human elite. (Many of whom may even be reptilian shape-shifters in human form, according to some sources, like David Icke and others... - Branton)

One of the men who was hit the hardest (by the horrifying stories emerging from out of the Dulce underground base) was William Randolph Leathers. Born in St. Louis Missouri . A graduate of Yale in 1941, he served in the O.S.S. as a Captain during World War II, teaching map reading in Aberdeen, Maryland for much of the war. One of the members of the top secret task force that hit the secret German military facility in Afghanistan in 1945, he had been a close friend of The Dutchman from that time, moving to Greenbrae, in Marin County,

California, in 1967 to be part of the headquarters team for I.S. (his cover was as an employee with the John Hancock Life Insurance Co.) Captain Leathers had lost his wife in 1971, and identified with several of the husbands and fathers of victims (he had four children of his own) for his own reasons (Captain Leathers died on October 22, 2001, at age 83). It would be Leathers who worked with the National Reconnaissance Office (NRO) satellite photos, U2 and SR-71 photos, and military maps of the area until all of the major portals to the Dulce Complex were spotted and marked. He would lead one of the assault teams himself.

Having turned 60 in 1978, Captain Leathers would be the oldest member of the assault team, to take an active role in the attack.

Most of the troops would come from three sources: The Delta Force, USAF-SOC, and the NSA Department "Z".

The U.S. Army's 1st Special Forces Operational Detachment-Delta (SFOD-D) would be one of two of the U.S. government's principle units tasked with counter terrorist operations outside the United States (the other being Naval Special Warfare Development Group, better known as SEAL team 6). Delta Force was created by U.S. Army Colonel Charles Beckwith in November 19th 1977 in direct response to numerous, well-publicized terrorist incidents that occurred in the 1970s. From its beginnings, Delta was heavily influenced by the British SAS, a philosophical result of Colonel Beckwith's year-long (1962-1963) exchange tour with that unit...

The Delta Force at Bragg was already considered the best special operation training facility in the world. After the assault on Dulce, the CQB indoor training range would be given the ominous nick-name, "The House of Horrors", in memory of what could not be remembered.

Most important; the Delta Force had their own fleet of helicopters (the aviation platoon). Painted in civilian colors and fake registration numbers, the helicopters could deploy with Delta operators and mount gun pods to provide air support as well as transportation, while not being easy to spot as 'military' units from the ground. It was decided that these air units, after delivering Delta Operators to several locations for forced entry into the facility, would come in with the NSA "Z-Team" as air support in the assault on the main landing port.

The Air Force Special Operation Command (AFSOC) would be in charge of taking and holding the main 'landing port'. The job of AFSOC "operators" was to quickly turn a given patch of hostile terrain into a fully functional airfield. Sometimes this meant a stealthy attack by motorcycle and ATV. Other times it meant cleaning out hostile forces by whatever means was necessary. In years to come, an AFSOC Special Tactics (ST) combat controller might have used a Special Operations Forces Laser Marker (SOFLAM) to create a spot where a laser-guided bomb could aim and neutralize the enemy; but in 1979 they had to do that with manpower...

Performing a diversified job required a diversified range of combat hardware. Air Force ST operators carried a variety of small arms, including the M9 9mm pistol with sound suppresser, the Remington 870 12-ga. shotgun, the M203 stand-alone 40mm grenade launcher, the M4A1 SOPMOD (Special Operations Peculiar Modification) 5.56mm carbine, and the M249 5.56 SAW (Squad Automatic Weapon). By making extensive tactical use of night vision gear, AFSOC's airborne capabilities were provided by the 16th Special Operations Wing, which is based at Hurlburt Field, Florida, and by units of Special Operations Groups at RAF Mildenhall, England. These wings had been the long-time vision of Major Ellis L. Richards, Jr., and others like him, and the Dulce Battle would be the first time they were used fully in combat.

But because of the special problems of entry into the Dulce facility, normal helicopter attack would not work. As well trained as they were, to attempt a landing into the hanger area of the facility would have been suicidal.

The Dulce landing ports were set up to accept the "lightcraft" and other Mass Accelerator Beam (MAB) Riders used by the Greys to transport from planet to orbital pick-up points. These craft generated magneto-hydrodynamic thrust, driven by microwaves and pulsed lasers, to accelerate the classic "flying saucers" up to altitudes of 50 kilometers and accelerations that easily allowed orbital velocities. This made the human-style of heavy-lift chemical rockets an expensive folly, and allowed the aliens Earth-to-orbit travel at will for a relatively low cost.

It also gave the human forces a way into the facility.

Because an infrastructure of orbiting stations were used to reflect energy from a solar-power station hidden on the Dark Side of the Moon, there were a number of ways to track such a ship. The lightcraft focused the microwave energy to create an "air spike" that deflected oncoming air - that could be tracked. And electrodes on the vehicle's rim that ionized air and formed part of the thrust-generating system could be seen by real-time cameras (and even the human eye at close ranges). Thus, it was planned that one of the attack teams would enter the facility when the main port's doors were open for an incoming lightcraft.

This was not going to be an easy stunt. Sensors around the area set off an alarm if anything got too close to the doors, not to mention warn the operators of any air or space vehicle that got too close. The mouth was too small for anything larger than a good sized helicopter, but helicopters would be too slow to reach the doors before the base defensive systems went off. And once inside the port area, any attack force would be likely overwhelmed by the base defenders - unless, whatever craft was used could carry a number of heavy automatic weapons, and land a large number of attackers at one time.

The Greys were quite content that no such craft existed in the human military inventory. And not even the Reptoids had a craft that could be used under all of the required conditions, that wouldn't be spotted long before it could reach the port.

What they hadn't counted on was one, single, experimental aircraft, that was still so secret that it had never been entered on any inventory list.

Manufactured by the Bell Corporation, the X-22 was a 'research' craft, with some interesting abilities. The first successful V/STOL VSS (Variable Stability System) aircraft, this strange mix of wings, jets, and huge ducted props might not have been pretty, but it was perfect for the mission needs of the Dulce Attack Force...

Because of the lack of time, the only man involved who also had the skill to fly the X-22 under such combat conditions was Captain Mark Richards. Thus he was chosen to lead Combat Assault Team (CAT) Three, that would be responsible for attacking the main landing port - and hold it long enough for other teams to land in conventional helicopters and for the evacuation of CAT's and victims when the attack was concluded.

According to records, Captain Richards had no more than 12 hours flying the X-22 before he took it into combat.

While the attack teams were being organized and trained, the attack itself was being planned by the men responsible for the situation. Objectives and alternative were picked, including a nuclear option in case the manned attack failed. Astronaut David Griggs was chosen to go with CAT-3 to make an attempt to 'loot' one of the alien space ships, while astronaut Ronald Ervin McNair went in as Richards' co-pilot and "laser weapons expert" (the fact that he was a black belt in Karate also came in highly helpful before the event was over). Astronaut Lieutenant Colonel Ellison S. Onizuka (USAF) and Colonel Stuart Allen Roosa (USAF) also went in as members of CAT-3 to gather information, and hopefully escape with alien ships or equipment, with Colonel Roosa commanding the Material Acquisition Team (MAT). None of their efforts could be of value, of course, unless the attack plan worked.

To make sure of success, the full information gathering ability of several top-secret departments within the NSA was turned loose on Dulce. Facts were gathered from sources far and wide, including everything from sightings listed in newspapers to interviews with people who helped to build the facility.

John V. Chambers, a Kentfield, CA resident...spent his working life in management and finance of large engineering construction projects...It would be Chambers, who had been involved with the Bechtel work at Dulce and other top secret government projects, who would be contacted by the forces that intended to attack Dulce, and became convinced to aid them in their effort...

It would be Mr. Chambers who would mention a number of weak points in the Dulce systems that would allow an attack to have a much better chance of success...It was Chambers who pointed out major weak points for the aliens...It seemed that the aliens had reason to worry about a number of the germs found outside the facility, and that some of the alien species were highly vulnerable to a number of human-passed diseases..."

The germs and bacteria that are everywhere on the planet, that humans and other mammals have (for the most part) developed ways to cope with, can offer great threat to aliens and their life forms. Earth dust, or bacteria blowing on the winds, can be deadly to a life form that has no resistance to such things. What humans refer to as 'hay fever' can be just as deadly to a creature that is having a difficult time 'breathing' in the Earth's oxygen rich atmosphere.

It was quickly realized that if the filters used to make Earth's 'air' more acceptable for the aliens could be disabled, many of the enemy would soon be sick and unable to continue to fight, and a large number might simply die on the spot!

Again, for lack of time, Lieutenant Colonel Onizuka took on the extra duty of leading a secondary team inside the main landing port once CAT-3 had secured the area - to disable the central air filter exchange that was next to the landing area. He created the title of Filter Assault Team (FAT) for his group, with his customary smile.

As the intelligence gathering expanded, a number of shocking facts were uncovered. In 1947, the Dutchman had been involved with Admiral Byrd in the attack of the last Nazi base at the South Pole.

Now he and others would come to better understand the connections that elite humans had developed with aliens, from the days of the Nazi efforts to modern times. This included helping the aliens to build secret bases all over the Earth (including the base at the South Pole, and the facility at Dulce), aiding in the abduction of young women for alien research and pleasure needs, and the addition of more pollution to the planet's atmosphere to bring on global warming and make the Earth more friendly to alien life forms.

One of the most shocking finds was the extent of the alien underground base-and-transportation network. While tube-trains had been expected, the vast bases that had been created came as a shock to even the best informed officers...

The reason such bases became more important now was that the human forces had to quickly find out where every base was that might react to an attack on Dulce, and how long it would take before they might send rescue forces. Another question was, how would they react in general? Might they attack humanity in some more deadly fashion than simply abducting a few thousand females a year? In the end it became clear that because of divisions in alien intentions, there was little organization between groups. Like a number of competing collages at a ruin, for the most part they were only interested in their own little outpost and research...

As for the rank-in-file men who took part in the mission, most of the names will be avoided to protect those men who are still alive (as of 2001, there aren't many still living), and those who are still involved as military operatives in one service or another. Men of the USAFSOC and Delta Force are some of the best trained warriors anywhere on the planet, and were more than ready for the challenge - even if nothing could have made them ready for what they would find once they got into the facility. There are a few general things to know about such men.

If one's self-esteem was fragile and required constant positive reinforcement, then a career in any of the organizations was definitely not for that person. Consider a typical Delta Force training exercise held in The Shooting House, where manikin terrorists held a real live "volunteer" hostage. The goal: Destroy the terrorists without harming the hostage, who happened to be a Delta Force trainee. Of course, for special missions, the 'terrorist' manikin could be replaced by a 'Grey' alien one.

Command Sgt. Major Eric L. Haney had been there for the formation of the elite group in 1978, being there for some of the first missions and the grueling training... "Within the next ten minutes, the door would be blown in and four of my classmates would assault the room using the close-quarter battle techniques we had learned. Bullets would rain throughout the room and someone would be firing live rounds within inches of my head. If they missed a single terrorist or hit me by mistake, the team would fail this phase of training... I sincerely wanted them to pass the exam," Haney would write in his 2001 book, Inside Delta Force: The Story of America's Elite Counter-terrorist Unit (Delacorte Press).

Of course, one got to participate in this practice session only if one successfully completed torturous training that culminated in a rugged 40-mile hike across the steep mountains of North Carolina, a 50-pound rucksack and a machine gun strapped on your back. Haney's description of that 18-hour test of his physical and mental stamina was one of many excellent narrative highlights in his account.

Haney, an Army Ranger when he was handpicked to try out for the elite unit, was one of 12 men out of 163 who made it to the level of Delta Force Operator. The new Delta Force members then "disappeared" from the more visible military units. "We operated like guerrillas. Or terrorists. Because the reality was, in order to become experts at counter-terrorism, we had to first become expert terrorists," he wrote.

While Haney did not mention the Dulce mission, he did include the failed attempt to rescue Americans held hostage in Tehran in which eight American military personnel died. Other missions included some of the world's toughest places, such as faction-torn Beirut in 1981 to guard the U.S. Embassy; quelling rebel insurgencies in Central America, including fighting Cuban guerrillas in Grenada; and protecting ambassadors, presidents, CEOs, celebrity prisoners and the offspring of all of the above. This was not accomplished without killing people, a task that Haney described in chilling detail.

Like most of the men involved in the Dulce attack, Haney was the kind of guy you wanted on your side in a street fight: skilled, intelligent and disciplined, but distrustful of the motives of some authority figures, especially career-climbing colonels and D.C., bureaucrats...

With Beckwith, Leathers and Donlon leading the three land-force CATs, the SOC men would be attacking under the command of a man most had never fought beside, but whom most had heard about...

Now, for the mission against Dulce, they were under the command of the Dutchman's son, who was something of a legend in his own right in the black ops circle. Two things were beyond question: the younger Richards had proven himself in combat, and he had never asked his men to do anything he wasn't ready to do, or left any behind. While his missions had almost always been so top secret that nobody knew details, the rumors and trail of evidence was more than clear to any in the know. The only problem for the command chain was his reputation for being something of a loose cannon when it came to following orders that he didn't think were in the best interest of his men or the mission - A fact that just made him more popular with his men.

In a typical command move on his part, as he sat in the X-22 with his troops ready to take off on what looked to many to be their last mission, he recited the prayer/poem; "I Am A Commando" to his men - their motto more than his -

"As my brother Commandos before me, I am proud to step into history as a member of the Air Force Special Operations Command.

"I will walk with pride with my head held high, my heart and attitude will show my allegiance to God, country and comrades. When unable to walk another step, I will walk another mile. With freedom my goal, I will step into destiny with pride and the Air Force Special Operations Command."

As he powered up the X-22, and gave the order for the helicopters to follow, he pushed the strange tilt-rotor aircraft to its flight limits in a wild high speed bank over the runway to impress the troops still on the ground - and set the tone for the mission. Over the earphones and speakers came first his voice, then the voice of the team members with him in the X-22, singing the Air Force hymn; "Up and Away, Into the Wild Blue Yonder..."

"We couldn't very well let that bunch smash open the Gates of Hell without the rest of us being right behind them," said one USAF helicopter pilot.

Timing was everything, with the X-22 taking the first wave of CAT-3 racing over the desert at over 250 miles-per-hour with the bottom of its rotor tubes missing the rocks by less than twenty feet at times. They had to hit the main landing port as an expected ship landed, as CAT-1 and CAT-2 came in on cargo tube trains several levels underground. CAT-4 was going to hit with a SEAL team coming through a water intake as the main group hit a small support hatch that would allow them to open another hatch to allow the SEAL team in. Everything, however, revolved around the success of CAT-3's attack in the main landing port, as they had to remove the main security control room and the 'sonic' weaponry systems that were controlled from there.

The X-22 came in as planned, racing over the badlands at over 200 mph while less than 20 feet off the sand. Five miles behind her was the main assault force being flown in heavy Air Force helicopters. The timing had to be perfect, hanging on the timely arrival of a large disk-like vehicle that was a known and expected cargo shuttle from space.

As observed, the main landing port "blanketing" holographic projectors were turned off, and the entry 'blast doors' were opened for the landing shuttle. Witnesses said that Richards' brought the X-22 so tightly that it's landing gear missed touching the top of the moving disk by only inches, lowering his roaring craft with the disk until he had cleared the upper support girder-system. Then the X-22 shot around the side of the shuttle, using it to block any attack by the main gun mounts of the landing port. The X-22 fired its Hellfire rockets to smash two gun blisters on the closer side of the port, as it landed on the roof of the main port control facility.

The attack was textbook, with the CAT-3 forces blowing an entry into the control tower and taking full control of that facility within 55 seconds of the X-22 breaching the port. Hovering, the X-22 continued to use its rockets and guns to rake any enemy weapons in the port area, silencing them before the Air Force started to enter the open port doors.

It was Ted Cochran of San Rafael, CA, who had been an Air Force helicopter rescue commander in the HH-43 Huskies based in Saigon in the height of the Vietnam conflict. Licensed since the age of 18 as a pilot, Cochran also served with the Air Force in Europe, where he had participated in the recovery of the lost thermonuclear weapon in Palomares, Spain. On one of his last helicopter missions before his legal retirement from the USAF, he was part of the recovery force for the Apollo 9 Mission after the first moon landing in 1969.

Returning to California, he got a master's degree in communications from Stanford University in 1972, and became a well-known film maker. A sailor, outdoorsman and aviator, Cochran combined his spirited passions into a career that allowed him to share his adventures with film audiences. His best known film was Island of the Bounty, about an international sailing expedition that traced the 1789 route of the famed HMS Bounty mutineers to Pitcairn Island in the South Pacific...

At age 39, Cochran was in his prime and had been more than willing to accept the request for his help as a helicopter pilot in some event like the Dulce Mission. The fact that he was a long-time friend of the Richards' family seemed to have something to do with his involvement as well. Indeed, it was rumored that he had taught the Dutchman how to fly the big HH-43 Huskies, and had flown in black ops' missions with the Dutchman's son several times before. He was one of the first names to be considered as a pilot.

It was Cochran who led the USAF AFSOC helicopters in, bringing his bird in fast and putting her down on the main floor of the chamber, where the troops would have the cover of a nearby disk as they ran for the nearby passenger entry hatch.

Seeing that the landing disk was now trying to escape, Richards landed on its edge and kicked the props of the X-22 into full down draft, nearly flipping the disk. Fighting to regain control of the X-22, he was forced to make a hard landing on a nearby pad, sending four more rockets into the shuttle forcing it to crash onto the two parked triangle-craft that were known to be fighter-type vehicles.

Although the men of CAT-3 were now taking heavy weapons fire from a number of directions in the landing port, they had disabled the main weapons pods, and the sonic systems for the whole facility, allowing the other teams to attack from different directions and locations. Holographic image systems were shut off, so that entry ports, airshafts, and other systems that were normally hidden now became fully exposed.

An alien security team had managed to close the main doors into the central HUB, and the first two men who attempted to get explosives close enough to damage the huge blast doors were cut down by enemy fire. Taking heavy damage, the X-22 rolled forward, and from less than 40 yards fired her remaining rockets. The resulting explosion blew the doors open, and wiped out any aliens on the other side for a hundred feet.

Forced to feather the now burning engines of the X-22, Richards took command of one of CAT-3's attack teams, and led the attack through the still smoking entry into the main central HUB, as other teams attacked from other directions.

The multi-leveled facility at Dulce, with its central HUB controlled by an extensive base security force, proved far more extensive and complex than the human attackers had been ready to cope with in the original plan. Information sources like Thomas (Castello) had clearance levels that did not allow them to know the full scope of the operation. His ULTRA-7 clearance granted him knowledge of seven (known) sub-levels - there were more. Most of the aliens supposedly were on levels 5, 6 and 7 - but there were more. There also was a more vast network of shuttle connections under the ground than expected; extending into a global network that had not been reported - providing escape routes and entry ports for rapidly deployed additional security forces that had not been expected.

In a report filed in early 1980, believed by a number of CIA sources to have been written by Brigadier General Aderholt, the author states:

"What those young men did was nothing less than the stuff of legend. Against overwhelming numbers and technology, they fought from Level 1 (containing the garages and hangers) down into the bowels of the enemy base. Portions of the combat took, and held, the Level 2 ports where tunnel shuttles and disc maintenance areas would have allowed enemy reinforcements to enter, while the main force charged forward towards Level 6, and 'Nightmare Hall,' to rescue the thousands of human victims kept there."

They were not ready for what they found in Level 6. Reports spoke of multi-armed and multi-legged humans and cages (and vats) of humanoid bat-like creatures as tall as 7-feet. The aliens had learned a great deal about genetics, things both useful and frightening. And most of it had been learned at the cost of human suffering and lives.

Captain Leathers' flight reached Level 7 first, blowing the main HUB entrance open and neutralizing the security force there with extreme prejudice in less than 45 second. On entering the security station, they realized the extent of the facility for the first time, finding systems for watching, and controlling, over 30,000 captives on that one level (alone), and the control and security systems for moving the captives to "testing facilities" and "pleasure centers" in over 62 different locations - where another 4,600 captives were currently kept.

Captain Leathers' report to I.S. would mention the moment:

"I looked out over holographic images of scenes of horror that are impossible to express in words, and a zoo of human being in various states of health and mental condition. Seeing images of young women being tortured at that very moment, all I could think of were my own daughters for several moments. Then I collected my wits, and gave the order to move forward to release as many of the victims as we could."

While the original mission plan had called for the teams to attack, smash as much of the enemy facility as they could, and withdraw in less than half an hour, the introduction of so many human victims added a new dimension to the problems at hand. While none of the officers in charge will admit to who made the order, recorded radio communications, and eyewitness reports, seem to suggest that Aderholt allowed the young Richards to change the mission demands as the numbers of "savable" victims became more apparent.

Captain Leathers' I.S. report reads:

"It wasn't like we had choices. We couldn't leave those poor girls behind alive. We knew that any that we didn't evacuate we were going to have to terminate. Our problem was simply numbers. Thousands of aliens trying to kill us. Thousands of human females screaming for help.

Thousands more so far gone that we knew we would have to leave them behind. Thousands of enemy troops starting to arrive on the subway trains. We just weren't set up for a mass evacuation. The sub tube back to New York, and one to Mexico, seemed to still be open, so we started loading girls into tube trains and shooting them off as soon as we knew our forces were in control of the stations at the other ends. We blew two air shafts wide open, so a couple squads could get girls out that way into the fresh air where hopefully our people could pick them up. CAT-4 took a real beating as they fought to keep alien reinforcements from entering the main sub tube stations. There is no doubt in my mind that we stayed in the facility too long, but at the time it was very hard to leave those poor young women behind. You knew that everyone you failed to send out in front of you was going to die, and soon."

  Exactly one hour after the X-22 had first attacked the main port entry, Aderholt ordered a full recall. David Griggs and R.E. McNair had by then managed to get two alien craft airborne - one disk-craft and one of the highly advanced triangle fighter-craft - and were running for Area 51. Roosa's men also had managed to get a huge disk-shuttle moving, in which over 3,600 human females had been loaded and were now being taken to a safe base.

The human attack teams were now withdrawing behind walls of smoke and set explosions. One of the frightening bits of equipment that the MAT men had found, but been forced to leave behind, was a type of "Cell-Electrostatic-Disruption" (CED) device - a weapon that could be set to disrupt the cells of a living creature at a subatomic level, thus killing everything living in an area while not doing much harm to any structures or equipment. To make sure there would be no survivors left in the facility, that device was set by the MAT technicians to go off shortly after the full withdrawal of the attack teams.

Lieutenant Colonel E.S. Onizuka, who had led the Filter Attack Team, managed to repair the X-22's battle damage before taking command of a captured alien triangle fighter-craft. As the wounded Richards fought a running retreat with the last of the rescued females and the survivors of CAT-4 and CAT-3, Ontzuka provided cover fire from the alien fighter-craft. This gave Richards the time to reach and restart the X-22 as Colonel Donlon loaded the last victim as he and two of his men fought off attacking alien shock troops.

Nearly overwhelmed, the human fighters in the X-22 would have likely not made it into the air if at that moment several battle craft hadn't darted into the port facility and started to lay down a brutal fire pattern against the other aliens.

While one can only guess at the reasons for this sudden aid, it has long been reported that the Dutchman, and his son, had highly questionable off-world contacts. From eyewitness accounts of the battle craft, one had the symbols on its wings of what human experts in the field suggest marked the craft as belonging to something like a 'prince' of a 'royal house'. Whatever the case, the Reptile battle craft fought on the side of the humans (indeed, two of their craft were lost in the battle), and gave the X-22 and Ontzuka's fighter-craft and the last two helicopters the chance to escape.

Seventy-two minutes, 14 seconds, after the attack had started, the X-22 and the Reptile battle craft with princely markings cleared the landing port's blast doors and dashed for safety. Explosions from dozens of set bombs started to blow up enemy craft as they took off, and thirty-five seconds after they cleared the doors, the CED went off, causing every life-form - alien and human - left inside the facility, to demolecularize on a subatomic level. Only a few in the heavily shielded lowest shelter levels survived.

The human female survivors were taken to several top secret military bases where they were "deprogramed" and "rehabilitated" so that they could be slowly farmed back into society with no memory of what they had suffered.

As the mysterious "Commander X" stated:

"...From my own intelligence work within the military, I can say WITH ALL CERTAINTY that one of the main reasons the public has been kept in total darkness about the reality of UFOs and 'aliens', is that the truth of the matter actually exists TOO CLOSE TO HOME TO DO ANYTHING ABOUT. How could a spokesman for the Pentagon dare admit that five or ten thousand feet underground EXISTS AN ENTIRE WORLD THAT IS 'FOREIGN' TO A BELIEF STRUCTURE WE HAVE HAD FOR CENTURIES? How could, for example, our fastest bomber be any challenge to those aerial invaders when we can only guess about the routes they take to the surface; eluding radar as they fly so low, headed back to their underground lair? ...the 'Greys' or the 'EBEs' have established a fortress, spreading out to other parts of the U.S. via means of a vast underground tunnel system THAT HAS VIRTUALLY EXISTED BEFORE RECORDED HISTORY..."

All of the men involved in any of the attack teams were either 'mind wiped' or sworn to secrecy on pain of death, or terminated (...by higher-level insiders following the battle, self-serving politicians and 'elite' who had nothing to do with initiating the attack, but who had everything to do with suppressing any information concerning it after the fact. - Branton). Because the officers in charge were seen as heroes by many of the political right-wing that took control in Washington in 1981, most were protected by the changing political elite. Many of those who had either openly backed the alien cause, or had profited from it in one way or another, were forced to pull back from their position for nearly ten years. Only when George Bush Sr. became President were the aliens able to return, and then only in much smaller numbers.

The Battle of Dulce ended the alien hope for using the Earth as a breeding tank for a subspecies, or for their take-over of the planet at any time in the near future. While the Grey's restarted a breeding program in 1993, and some of the lower levels of the Dulce Facility were reopened by 1998, the numbers are in the tens' or hundreds rather than the thousands. And USAF Space Command now tracks all alien craft, with the constant threat that Top Secret

"Flights" can react and attack an otherworld enemy at any moment, with dramatic results...

Over 50 years of intense UFO interest, investigation, researching, evaluation, and theorizing by countless UFO aficionados have enabled modern field investigators to better examine, evaluate, and identify many of the unusual airborne objects that are being reported. Yet a small percentage of the reports continue to elude positive identification. Rumors of what took place at Dulce in 1979 have already been reduced to legend at the end of the 20th century. Indeed, the continued 'conmen' involved with such reports have helped the USAF cover the truth of events that took place at Dulce, and continue to aid in the effort to hide the ruined facility and those who took part in events there.

Men like intelligence officer William Cooper, who have become too loose with their knowledge of the truth, can be discredited in any number of ways, or terminated if they become too great a threat. It should be clear from their actions, and their willingness to challenge authority, that these men must never be allowed into such a position of power or authority again (or rather, such is the mindset of the human - or shapeshifting - elite). While the "Dutchman" was terminated in 1996, and his son will be in prison for the rest of his life, the mindset itself that created such men must be crushed if the human race is to know peace with the aliens (but then again, the elite & gray-alien version of 'peace' is more akin to 'assimilation' - Branton). The illusion of freedom that may be lost by those few who know what is really going on will be a worthy exchange for amazing technology that will come into the hands of the human elite (so they reason) that takes part in the new transfer. This may not take place easily, of course, until all human resistance has been removed either through retraining or through conquest. (This is the distorted reasoning of the 'elite' who would sell out our planet for their own selfish personal physical gain - Branton)

One of the key lessons to be learned from the Dulce Battle is as long as there are small, highly trained and well equipped human forces that can, may, or will go into action on their own accord to protect the people of the Earth, easy conquest of the planet becomes difficult. A departmentalized military, with some branches so Top Secret that even the political elite who rule the country aren't too sure of what is out there, is a threat to any enemy. At this time, there are arms of the USAF Space Command so Top Secret that no one in the Pentagon knows that they exist in anything but legend.

If humanity is to survive long enough for it to take a historic place in the civilized social structures of the universe, they must either defend themselves from any life-form that would harm them or their planet, or surrender themselves to some sort of interplanetary police force that will protect them. At this time, only rumors of such a police force have reached those in the know, leaving self-defense as the only real option. The men who attacked the Dulce Facility in 1979 understood that reality, and took the task of defending humanity into their own hands. One can only make subjective guesses at what might have happened if they had not done what they did.

******* ******* *******

PLAYERS

BRIGADIER GENERAL H.C. ADERHOLT: Mission Commander.

COLONEL CHARLES BECKWITH: Commander of Delta Force and CAT-1.

J.V. CHAMBERS: Engineer for Bechtel.

WILLIAM COOPER: Intelligence Officer.

COLONEL R.H.C. DONLON: Commander CAT-4.

DAVID GRIGGS: Astronaut, liberated UFO.

COMMAND SGT. MAJOR E.L. HANEY: Delta Force Commander/Writer

GENERAL R.T. HERRES: Commander of USAF Communications Command at Scott Air Force Base, Ill.

KARL GORDON HENIZE: Organized mission flight teams.

GENERAL D.C. JONES: Chairman Joint Chiefs of Staff.

CAPTAIN W.R. LEATHERS: Commander CAT-2.

R.E. McNAIR: Laser expert, liberated UFO.

LIEUTENANT COLONEL E.S. ONIZUKA: Commander of FAT, liberated UFO.

ROSS PEROT: Helped to fund the mission.

MAJOR E.L. RICHARDS, JR.: 'The Dutchman' - Commander in Chief of the Dulce Mission, Head of I.S.

CAPTAIN M. RICHARDS: Commander of CAT-3.

COLONEL S.A. ROOSA: Commander MAT.

EDWIN WILSON: Helped to fund the mission.

TERMS

CAT = Combat Assault Team.

FAT = Filter Attack Team.

MAT = Material Acquisition Team.

IS = International Security

VAT = Victim Assistance Team.

As with most things in the field of UFO study it is hard to know what is truthful and what is the wildest of fiction. This author was on the ground in Dulcwe, saw the Black Helicopters and the entrance to the underground base. I also interviewed a number of witnesses who in my estimation were telling the truth. Whatever may be ficitonal, there is most definitely a Dulce Base. Who staffs it is anyone's guess.

INDEX

1

1954 Greada Treaty, 81

A

Aderholt, Brigadier General, 186, 207
Adventure Radio, 32, 75
Aerial Phenomena Research Organization. *See* APRO
Aerospacial in France, 85
Ancestral Man, 12
Ancestral Woman, 12
Ancient Aliens Season 2, Episode 4, 32
Ancient Gods, 4
Angel of Death, 4
Animal Mutilations, 23
Archuleta Mesa, 15, 23, 27, 32, 35, 37, 39, 70, 117, 175
Area 51, 50, 61, 65, 83, 134, 135, 176, 210
Arizona, Page, 65, 135

B

Barkun, Michael, 20, 31
Battle of Dulce, 214
Bechtel, 22, 23, 85, 195, 217
Beckwith, Colonel Charles, 189
Bell Corporation, 193
Bennewitz, Paul, 19, 27, 69
Berlitz, Charles, 30
Bethlehem Steel, 84
Bielek, Al, 79, 127, 131, 134, 157, 166
Black Budget, 79

Blue Planet Project, 61
Boeing Aerospace, 85

C

Castello, Thomas Edwin, 63
Cheney, Dick, 23
Colorado, Colorado Springs, 65
Colorado, Creed, 65
Comanches, 12
Commander X, 213
Conspiracy Theory, 32
CONTACT: THE PHOENIX PROJECT, 119
Cooper, William, 48, 215
Coyote Canyon Test Area, 29

D

DARPA, 43, 44, 45, 50
Defense Advanced Research Projects Agency. *See* DARPA
Delta Force, 20, 32, 87, 164, 189, 190, 198, 199, 200, 217, 218
DELTA FORCE, 177, 187
Delta Group, 24
Donlon, Colonel Roger H.C., 187
Doty, Richard, 30
Draco-Reptoids, 46, 57
Drayer, Cynthia, 96, 104
Dulce Attack Force, 194
Dulce Base, 21, 23, 24, 29, 30, 32, 55, 56, 58, 59, 61, 65, 75, 76, 81, 95, 119, 184, 190, 220
Dulce Battle, 191
Dulce Complex, 189
Dulce Conference, 61
Dulce Facility, 64, 181, 186, 192, 214

Dulce Firefight, 61
Dulce Labs, 54
Dulce Lake, 23, 39
Dulce Landing Ports, 192
Dulce Papers, 41, 64
Dulce Report, 61
Dulce Symbol, 48
Dulce systems, 195
Dulce underground facility, 63
Dulce Underground Labs, 68
Dulce Underground UFO Base Conference, 35
Dulce War, 75
Dulce Wars, 57
Dutchman, 177, 180, 188, 197, 201, 205, 212, 215, 219

E

Earth Defense Headquarters, 174
EG&G, 83, 85
El Vado, 21, 59

F

Faber, Chief Raynard, 14, 36
Flash Gun, 48
Four Corners Region, 24
Freedom of Information Act, 78

G

Gates of Hell, 202
Greys, 37, 40, 43, 64, 73, 76, 82, 152, 156, 178, 179, 180, 182, 192, 193, 213
Griggs, David, 194, 210
Groom Lake installation, 50
Gunderson Steel Fabrication, 83

H

Haney, Command Sgt. Major Eric L., 199
Hansen, Myrna, 28, 70, 71

Henize, Karl Gordon, 187
Howard Hughes Medical Institute, 68
Howe, Linda Moulton, 71
HUB, 39, 64, 206, 207, 208
Human Genome Project, 46, 56
Human-Aura research, 51

I

I G Farben, 85
INTRUDERS, 184

J

Jicarilla Apache Reservation, 9, 114

K

Kirtland Air Force Base, 29

L

Lear, John, 20, 31, 71
Leathers, William Randolph, 188
Lévesque, Tal, 184
Livermore Berkeley Labs, 23, 47
Lorimar Aerospace, 85
Los Alamos, 20, 22, 43, 56, 58, 60, 64, 68, 117, 178
Los Alamos National Laboratory, 45

M

Manzano Nuclear Weapons Storage Facility, 29
McDonnell Douglas, 85
McNair, Ronald Ervin, 194
Mitsubishi Industries, 85
MJ 12, 176
Moore, William, 30
Morrison and Knudson, 83
MUFON, 61

N

National Institute of Health, 68
National Science Foundation, 68
National Security Agency. *See* NSA
National Security Council. *See* NSC
Native American legends, 107
Navajo Dam, 21, 58
New Mexico, Carlsbad, 65
New Mexico, Chama, 62
New Mexico, Datil, 65
New Mexico, Dulce, 9, 11, 14, 19, 20, 21, 22, 23, 24, 27, 30, 31, 32, 33, 35, 36, 37, 39, 41, 46, 47, 48, 53, 55, 56, 58, 59, 61, 64, 65, 67, 68, 69, 71, 72, 73, 75, 76, 77, 82, 95, 97, 102, 104, 108, 114, 117, 124, 125, 134, 135, 151, 164, 175, 176, 177, 178, 179, 180, 181, 185, 187, 188, 195, 197, 201, 205, 207, 215, 216, 217, 219
New Mexico, Farmington, 38
New Mexico, Rio Arriba County, 9
New Mexico, Roswell, 21
New Mexico, Sandia', 65
New Mexico, Taos, 65
New World Order, 40, 49, 77, 80, 100, 123, 125, 129, 131, 138, 161, 166, 167
Nightmare Hall, 46, 56, 60, 66, 208
NSA, 157, 176, 177, 189, 190, 195
NSC, 176

O

Oklahoma City bombing, 119
Omega Press, 3
Onizuka, Lieutenant Colonel Ellison S., 195

P

PANDORA'S BOX, 170

Perot, Ross, 187
Philadelphia Experiment, 80, 97, 102, 166
Project Beta, 29

R

Rand Corporation, 63
Reptilian Race, 40
Reptilians. *See* Dracos
Reptoid, 42, 64, 67, 181, 182
Richards Jr., Major E.L., 187
Richards, Captain Mark, 177, 180, 187, 194
Roosa, Colonel Stuart Allen, 195
Ryder Trucks, 85

S

Sandia Base, 50
Sasquatch, 15, 24, 36, 37, 114, 116
Schneider, Otto Oscar, 80
Schneider, Phil, 71, 72, 75, 76, 77, 93, 95, 96, 123, 125, 134, 142, 150, 164
SEALS, 187

'Shadow Government, 22

S

skin walker, 108, 109, 110, 111
skin-walker, 107
Souder, Richard, 79
Star Wars, 85, 86
Steiger, Brad, 184
Subterrene, 22

T

Texas

El Paso, 3, 4, 5
The Jason Group, 50
Thomas C, 41
Tiller, Veronica E. Velarde, 12
Tilton, Christa, 24, 71
tube-shuttle, 20, 58

U

UFO Hunters, 32
Unidentified Flying Objects, 6
USAF Space Command, 186, 188, 214, 216

V

Valdez, Gabe, 69
Valerian, Val, 184

W

Wackenhut Security Systems,, 85
Wang. Connie, 4
Westinghouse, 85
Wild Horse Casino, 35, 36
Wilson, Edwin, 187

X

X-22, 193, 194, 201, 202, 203, 204, 206, 210, 211, 212

Y

Yellow Fruit, 23

www.ingramcontent.com/pod-product-compliance
Lightning Source LLC
Chambersburg PA
CBHW071610080526
44588CB00010B/1084